FINDING
CONTENTMENT

Donated By

Margaret and Blair Marriott

"The Lord gives wisdom, and from His mouth
come knowledge and understanding."
Proverbs 2:6

neil clark warren

FINDING
CONTENTMENT

Published in Nashville, Tennessee, by Thomas Nelson, Inc., Publishers, and distributed in Canada by Word Communications, Ltd., Richmond, British Columbia.

The Bible version used in this publication is THE NEW KING JAMES VERSION. Copyright © 1979, 1980, 1982, 1990, Thomas Nelson, Inc., Publishers.

Case studies are based on composites that have been fictionalized beyond recognition and are in no way intended to represent the actual people involved.

Library of Congress Cataloging-in-Publication Data

Warren, Neil Clark.
    Finding contentment / Neil Clark Warren.
       p.   cm.
    Includes bibliographical references.
    ISBN 0-7852-7234-8 (hc)
    ISBN 0-7852-7057-4 (pb)
    1. Contentment. 2. Authenticity (Philosophy) I. Title.
BJ1533.C7W35 1997
170'.44—dc21   97–26335
                                                     CIP

Printed in the United States of America.

1 2 3 4 5 6 BVG 02 01 00 99 98 97

DEDICATION

This book is dedicated to all courageous readers
who determine to break their habitual way of
settling for momentary happiness and choose to
pursue contentment by walking the road of
authenticity. May your lives overflow
with peace and serenity.

CONTENTS

ACKNOWLEDGMENTS

First, I want to acknowledge my editor and close friend, Keith Wall. He gave this project at least twice as much time as anyone could have expected. He is a master of the written word, and I repeat my determination never to write again without his full partnership.

Rolf Zettersten, publisher at Thomas Nelson, Inc., has parented this project from start to finish. Rolf listens with incredible precision, acts in a flash, and has better judgment than anyone else I know.

Janet Thoma has used her vast publishing experience to guide this entire effort. She has carefully stayed on top of every detail.

I wrote to twenty-five of my friends in the book's early stages and asked for their counsel about direction and perspective. They responded instantly with keen insight. I especially want to thank Nathan and Sue Braden, who gave so generously of their time and energy every time I contacted them.

My friends Howard and Nell Privett took an intense interest in every phase of the writing. This encouraged me more than they could know.

My partner and close friend Greg Forgatch gently and subtly stabilized my life through the demanding days of writing.

Lorrie Warren Forgatch and Luann Warren-Sohlberg gave me one idea after another relating to contentment.

You cannot read this book without being struck by the unusual importance of my clients to my thinking. Their stories are scrambled and coalesced, so that they will not recognize themselves, but they will see their contributions in a thousand ways.

As always, it was Marylyn Mann Warren who listened to nearly every word, encouraged me, questioned me, prayed for me every day I wrote, and labored to understand all the passion I have about this subject after all these years of trying to help my clients find wholeness.

Of course, I deeply thank all these people, but more than that, I wish for them the deep-down contentment about which they have helped me write.

part one

MOMENTARY HAPPINESS OR ENDURING CONTENTMENT?

chapter one

■

THE GRAND SEARCH

☐Everyone is searching for the secret of contentment.

I don't mean the secret to becoming fabulously rich, incredibly good-looking, or wildly successful in a career. Nor do I mean basking in the applause of thousands at Carnegie Hall, seeing your face on the cover of *Vogue*, or leading a Fortune 500 company. Nor, for that matter, do I mean being the most popular person in your group, driving a fancy car, owning a palatial house, or graduating at the top of your class—though we all know that millions of people pursue these goals ferociously.

The search I'm talking about is for *enduring* contentment, the kind of deep-down, soul-satisfying contentment that infuses your life with peace and serenity, gives you the freedom and energy to express yourself and follow your dreams despite what others may think, and allows you to fall asleep at night without fretting about what might have been.

The secret of contentment lies in discovering who in the world you are— and mobilizing your courage to be that person. The richest and deepest contentment is a natural result of achieving authenticity—that is, knowing yourself intimately, appreciating your unique gifts and abilities, and making choices moment by moment that demonstrate honor and respect for yourself.

Unfortunately, too many of us never locate our genuine selves. In the absence of our true identities, we frantically try to be the "somebody" we think we must be to please others. Our frustration at playing what we know to be a false role is matched only by our persistent anxiety that our lives will ultimately bring disillusionment and emptiness. Our most frequent response is to increase the pace—make more money, pursue more adventure, earn more degrees, climb higher on the corporate ladder, take more vacations to exotic locations.

The best we seem to do is to engage with the external world in a set of transactions designed to secure for us frequent, albeit superficial, "happiness surges." We leapfrog from one activity or relationship or purchase or job to the next in the quest for fulfillment. But these "rushes" of happiness are short-lived and incapable of satisfying us at a deep level. Short bursts of happiness, though, become the only goal available to us if we fail to define ourselves—to be authentic. Simply stated, enduring contentment is unattainable to people who remain lost from their true identities.

Instinctively, you know that small doses of happiness are a far stretch from contentment. Contentment has its roots way down at the center of yourself, where your consciousness is headquartered, where you perceive, think, feel, and dream. Happiness doesn't go nearly as deep. *Contentment* is almost always the consequence of your relationship with yourself, a consistent loyalty to the person you truly are. *Happiness* is far more superficial and is usually contingent upon something external to you, perhaps an encounter with another person, your experience at a party, a shopping spree, an exciting movie, maybe even an achievement in your career or an honor you receive.

■

OUR GOAL IS DEEP, GENUINE CONTENTMENT

As captured as we become by a frantic search for happiness surges, we seldom lose total touch with our deep hunger for contentment. We can deny, ignore, or disregard our nagging ache for true contentment, but it's always there. That's because at the center of our inner beings, we yearn for a quiet sense of satisfaction. We desperately long for a sustained feeling of peace—for some realization that we have encountered ourselves at a deep level and that we are finally at ease with who we are.

Almost everyone, I think, passionately longs for enduring contentment.

You may be experiencing in your own life this hunger or longing, which likely is expressed in one or more of these ways:

- You feel an all-too-frequent sense of boredom and emptiness.
- You find yourself surfing through the channels of your television set, almost frantically searching for something that will satisfy your inner hunger.
- Your job is chronically frustrating, but so was your last one.
- Your spouse is demanding but unexciting, and you wonder if you really belong together.

- Your spiritual interests are far less intense; in fact, they're almost nonexistent at times.
- You are too often lonely.

I recently broached the issue with dozens of people. In a single day, I asked 108 individuals whether they would rather be "immediately happy," "enduringly content," or "incredibly rich." Eighty-six of them told me they would choose "enduringly content," nineteen selected "immediately happy," and only three said "incredibly rich."

Many of these "subjects" asked me to define the words *content* and *happy*, but in each case, I said, "I simply want you to choose one of the three alternatives without any further definition of terms." By the end of the informal survey, it was obvious that the vast majority of participants agreed with me about the desire to be "enduringly content" rather than "immediately happy."

As you would expect, literally no one asked what it meant to be "incredibly rich." And however hard people may be trying to reach this state, the consistently popular choosing of the other two alternatives made it clear that the vast majority of people would rather be content than rich, even if they could be *incredibly* rich.

■

THE APPEAL OF ENDURING CONTENTMENT

One of the men in my "study," the husband of a woman who works in the office next to mine, explained why he chose "enduringly content" as his preferred inner state.

"During the last two years," he said, "I've become aware that I'm sometimes happy but seldom content. You know, there are many wonderful things happening in my life, but it still seems like there's something—some piece—missing."

I knew this man to be the vice president of a successful import-export business. What's more, he had achieved and acquired many of the things that would make others envious—a stable family, a beautiful house near the ocean, opportunities to travel, and a membership at an exclusive golf club. I asked him to tell me more, and he continued, speaking slowly and thoughtfully.

"Any happiness I experience seems to result from whatever's happening at the moment," he said. "If I go rock climbing with my son, I feel exhilarated. If I watch a great show or game on TV, I feel gratified. If I beat my handicap on the golf course, I'm ecstatic. If I close a big deal and the boss praises my work, I'm thrilled. I might even say that in those moments I'm happy."

Then he added the clincher: "But *contentment* is what I'm looking for—something deeper, more at the center of me, more lasting."

Contentment! That deep, inner condition of knowing that you have found yourself—and that you are courageously trying to be the person you were meant to be. The result of this noble effort is a profound sense of self-satisfaction and self-appreciation. This state of mind and heart is incredibly attractive to the vast majority of people. As confused as most men and women are about how to achieve it, there is widespread recognition that enduring contentment is the grand quest of the human experience.

■

AUTHENTICITY IS THE ONLY ROAD TO CONTENTMENT

The most fundamental idea in this book—and the idea I believe to be at the center of a great life—is that you can experience enduring contentment only when you have the courage to be deeply and profoundly your true self, the self you discover when you make careful and solid choices about your life all along the way. In other words, contentment will be forever elusive unless you learn to be authentic and genuine.

During my years of graduate work, I studied under renowned and learned professors who lectured on the search for contentment. I wrote papers on the emotional and psychological aspects of striving for well-being and inner peace. And through my education and years of psychological practice, I had become convinced that a link exists between authenticity and contentment. But as so often happens in life, an unexpected source taught me this lesson most powerfully. Ten years ago, a janitor named Julio Martinez clearly illustrated for me the connection between being authentic and enjoying contentment.

I had spoken with Julio many times, since he often arrived at my office pushing his cleaning cart just as I was locking up to go home. We had swapped jokes, speculated together on how the Dodgers would do that season, and occasionally talked about our families. Late one night when I was still at my desk trying to meet a manuscript deadline, Julio engaged me in a conversation—a conversation I didn't have time for, but one that turned out to be unusually important.

"You know, Doc," he said, "my thirteen-year-old son, Michael, was arrested the other night for shoplifting. I'm torn up about it. My wife is brokenhearted. We feel sick about it. I thought about calling you to see if you could help us."

"That's really too bad, Julio," I told him. "I know how hard you've worked to bring your kids up right. I can imagine that it devastated both of you."

"We were totally shocked," he continued. "Michael is a great kid, and he's been doing real well in school. He's our oldest child, and we count on his help with the three younger kids."

"Why do you think he shoplifted?" I asked. "What seemed to be going on with him?"

"Well, he stole some sneakers and a warm-up jacket," Julio answered. "He says that the kids at school make fun of him because he doesn't have the right kind of clothes—you know, the kind of *cool* clothes kids *have* to have. He said he just wanted to fit in. He's tired of being picked on and laughed at. But listen, Doc, we don't have money for things like that. I tried to explain to him that our rent and food take every penny I make. There's nothing left over."

"So Michael ended up stealing tennis shoes and a jacket so he could be like the other kids," I said. "I bet it's hard for him to go to school without the 'required equipment.' Those teenage years are tough, even under the best of circumstances. It's hard for a kid to feel all that embarrassment—"

"Don't get me wrong," Julio broke in. "I feel terrible that I can't buy him those things. I'd give anything if I didn't have to put him in a position like that."

By that time, Julio had tears in his eyes, and he was trying hard not to cry. "But my wife and I aren't so upset because Michael feels like an outsider," he continued. "We're upset because our boy stole to try to be someone he's not. You see, we're poor people, and that's just the way it is. Pretending that we're not won't get Michael anywhere. I tell my kids all the time, 'Be who you really are!' That's the only way to make it in this life. If you try to be someone you're not, you may impress other people, but you'll feel lousy about yourself. Michael let those other kids tempt him into being someone he's not."

My conversation with Julio lasted only a few minutes, but I became aware somewhere along the way that I was talking to an incredible man, a wise man, an obviously proud man. And he was telling me that the secret to a good life is your willingness to be authentic, to be genuine, to "be who you really are."

Julio's grief over his boy had little to do with broken laws and rules. He and his wife were sad that their son hadn't learned the great secret they had tried so hard to instill in him: Contentment at the center of your being comes with the courage to be the person you truly are— to simply be yourself—regardless of what people might think.

We should all be as perceptive as Julio Martinez!

■

AUTHENTICITY IS LIFE'S FIERCEST AND MOST CRITICAL BATTLE

Life involves a battle for who is going to be in charge of our lives. All kinds of insecure people would like to take control of our decision making, of our very personhood. (Even as you read this chapter, you'll probably think of a few in your life!) Most often these controllers are people in our closest circle—parents, siblings, spouse, boss, friends. If we allow them to do our choosing—to determine who we will be— they somehow feel more powerful, more secure, and better about themselves.

But if you give others control over your decision making, you will never become the person you were meant to be. You will most likely become the person *they* want you to be, but you will thereby become lost to yourself. This is, without question, the worst fate possible for any human being. For if you fail to captain your own ship through life, you will inevitably experience an inner emptiness. You are not being the person you were born to be. The immediate and long-term pain is excruciating. In this inauthentic state, you won't come near enduring contentment. Artificiality, superficiality, and emptiness will characterize your life.

Enduring contentment requires that you strongly resist every outside effort to take you over. You must wage an unrelenting battle. You have to stand resolutely at the center of yourself and make consistently wise decisions in every moment.

Getting yourself interpersonally free to function this way is massively difficult. If you refuse to give controllers the power they seek, they will almost always turn to punishing you in some way. They may laugh at you, exclude you, severely criticize you, withhold affection from you, or totally reject you.

So you must be persistently committed to making your own decisions about what is best for you. This commitment needs to emerge from a strong conviction that when you are true to the person you really are, you will indeed experience enduring contentment.

■

THE STRUGGLE CAN BE INTENSE

A few years ago, I saw a married couple for therapy—I'll call them Diane and Paul—who came with an issue that clearly illustrates my point. Paul was a graphic designer, and Diane taught kindergarten. Although they had many things going for them as a couple, the problem that brought them to my office was this: Paul was part of a group of heavy partyers—many of whom had been in his college fraternity. They threw a party or two every month, and Paul put a lot of pressure on Diane to go with him.

But Diane hated going! There was always a lot of drinking, loud music, and obnoxious joking. Partying like that just wasn't for her. She tried to attend without drinking much, but she felt uncomfortable, and she heard whispers that others resented her for not joining in. To complicate matters, rumors about sexual encounters between various members of the group had begun to surface. Although Paul had not been mentioned, Diane didn't trust him in the party atmosphere.

Paul did everything he could think of to get Diane to go with him. But she finally decided not to attend any more parties. She told Paul in the kindest way she knew, and she let him know that her decision was final. The way she described it to me later, Paul erupted.

"How can you be such a killjoy?" he yelled. "You want to stay home all the time and live a boring, pathetic life…well, that's not what I'm going to do!"

Just when she thought he had cooled down, he said, "You know what you are, Diane? A holier-than-thou! You don't like to drink, and you don't like my friends, so you stick your nose in the air and act like you're better than everyone else. Yeah, well, someday you'll be sorry you treated me and my friends like scum!"

It didn't take great therapeutic skill on my part to recognize that Paul was intent on revenge. How dare she make a decision for herself that took him out of control of her life?

When I saw Diane for an individual session following this blowup, she was worried that the marriage might not survive her authenticity. In fact, the conflict over the party-going was just one piece in a much larger puzzle. Paul controlled many aspects of Diane's life: what she wore, where she went, what kinds of friends she had. She was miserable—not just because of her marital problems, but because she felt stifled and suffocated. She finally reached her limit and drew the line at the party issue.

"This is the first time I've stood up for myself," she told me. "Always before, I just went along with what Paul wanted. But I got tired of it, you know? I mean, what about me? I need to listen to myself."

Bingo! I thought. *You'll never break free and attain real contentment until you're true to yourself and find the courage to be who you really are.*

Still, Diane's fears were not unfounded. Her stand had upset the equilibrium of her marriage, and Paul did not adjust easily to their new balance of power. As a matter of fact, I thought for a few months that Paul might bolt. But he eventually recognized—and took responsibility for—his role in this power play. He began to lighten up on his wife, and their relationship grew stronger. Diane told me she felt as if she had been released from a twenty-five-year prison sentence.

The kind of courage Diane displayed is often what it takes to be authentic. Sometimes you have to take enormous risks to discover who you are and, more important, *live out* who you are. To be the person you truly are, you have to be willing to face tremendous loss. You may permanently offend a close friend, cause a parent to distance herself from you, put your job in jeopardy, or lose an important account.

People intent on being authentic are called upon to make decisions every day that require courage. Some of these decisions are relatively minor, but others are monumental. In every situation that requires a choice to be authentic, there is the risk of loss in order to be true to one's deepest and best sense of what is right at the time.

In fact, men and women throughout history have had to pay with their very lives for their authenticity. Consider Abraham Lincoln, for instance. He could easily have avoided the bloody Civil War in which so many people were killed and injured. All he needed to do was give others control over his decision making. If he had followed the safe route, he could have undoubtedly saved his life. But by standing firm for what he was convinced was right, Lincoln eventually paid with all he had to pay.

Choosing to be authentic can be overwhelmingly risky. But here's the payoff: When you are authentic, you set yourself up for the deepest kind of enduring contentment. You discover the profound peace that accompanies a set of free and effective choices, the feeling of fulfillment and inner calm you have when you confidently know that you are fully capable of representing and standing by your deepest desires and your best judgment. The ground may be very rocky on the road to genuineness, but the ultimate reward for getting there is unbelievably satisfying. It is the reward that nearly all of us want more than any other.

■

THREE PEOPLE WHO FOUND ENDURING CONTENTMENT

I first met Marie at a seminar for singles where I was speaking. She was thirty-two years old at the time, and although she had never been married, she had been involved in two or three long-term relationships. During a break, she approached me to talk.

After a few introductory comments, she told me, "I'm convinced I'll never be content until I'm married."

I was impressed by her candor, but I thought she was dead wrong! So I said as gently as I could, "I couldn't disagree more. In fact, one of the main reasons people get married is that they are looking for *someone else* to complete them, to bring them fulfillment. When that doesn't happen, they figure they must have married the wrong person. So they search for another partner and repeat the cycle again."

I moved a little closer to make sure she was listening, then said, "Here's the bottom line: Marriage can be wonderfully enriching, but it is up to you, not someone else, to bring about your contentment."

Despite my best efforts, I sensed that she was unconvinced by what I'd said. After all, when a person gets captivated by a powerful idea, especially one that's consistently reinforced by our society, breaking free from it can be an incredible struggle.

Marie lived within a half hour of my office in the Los Angeles area, and one day she called for an appointment. I remembered her well from our brief conversation, and I welcomed the opportunity to work with her. At her first appointment, I asked why she was seeking my help.

"I'm terribly unhappy," she said, "and I'll never be satisfied until I get married!"

I knew I hadn't persuaded her!

"For some reason," she continued, "my relationships just don't work out. What I want more than anything in the world just hasn't happened for me. I need your help."

I certainly didn't want to dismiss the pain Marie felt over being single, but I knew that pain was a symptom of a deeper problem. I learned that she grew up with a controlling mother and that she had spent her childhood trying to fulfill Mom's expectations and demands. Marie's pattern of relating to others was to please them, to become whatever others wanted her to be. She never invested the time and energy in discovering who she was at the core of her being: her convictions, passions, likes, and dislikes. Consequently, she believed—as she had announced so boldly to me at the seminar—that she could not be content on her own. She thought something else was required, and the most likely "something else" she could think of was marriage.

As we worked together for seven months, two things began to happen. First, her focus moved from everyone around her (especially potential mates) to inside herself, and second, her fixation on getting married began to give way. She got involved in a local church, which encouraged her to pursue regular times of prayer and reflection. She started spending more time by herself rather than in her frantic pursuit of a man, and for the first time in her life, she became acquainted with herself. She became dedicated to the discovery and expression of her true self. As she did, her personal sense of worth grew.

Over those months, I watched Marie become emotionally healthy. She began to take responsibility for her decision making, and she let go of an idea that wouldn't work, an idea that had become a false god for her.

And I watched her become more and more content with her life. Marie became a substantially more attractive human being and prospective marriage candidate as she became a strong, contented person.

I was thrilled by her progress, and I told her so. "This is fantastic, Marie. You see what's happened? Even as you've let go of the idea that only a marriage partner can bring you contentment, you've put yourself in a much better position to have a happy, lasting marriage. And even if that doesn't happen, you have an incredibly fulfilling life ahead."

"I couldn't agree more," she said.

■

A SIMILAR THING HAPPENED TO A MINISTER I KNOW

We often assume that our leaders are squared away, that they are enduringly content on the basis of their authentic lives. While many are, this is not always the case. Some important people have become successful because of their exceptional gifts and talents rather than their emotional health. They have kept themselves relatively happy by pleasing and impressing other people on a continual basis. But they often reach a point in their lives when they discover that they are not content. They may be horribly miserable—even emotionally lost.

I have a minister friend who experienced this. He became pastor of one of the largest churches in America, but he suddenly realized in the middle of his grand life that he was virtually empty inside. He was addicted to the praise of others, and he never discovered how to achieve authenticity in his life. He relied on a strategy that everyone except him thought was working unusually well.

"Neil," he said during one of our long phone conversations, "I've accomplished everything I salivated over as a young seminary student. I'm leading a big, dynamic, influential church. Things are going well at home too. Sally and the kids are terrific. So why am I *trudging* through every day?"

After talking a few times to make sure I understood the situation, I said, "I encourage you to do something that you recommend to your parishioners but haven't really done yourself—spend time meditating and reflecting. It's critical that you break free from your addiction to the acclaim and approval of your church members. And the way to do that is to stand tall in the middle of your life, become a strong, independent decision maker, and get perfectly clear about your own strengths, weaknesses, motivations, goals, and so on. I guarantee that if you do this, you'll experience the greatest single feeling there is—contentment."

He struggled for months to become an authentic person, a man who operated from his center, who valued his convictions and ideas as much as the opinions and wishes of his parishioners. But the process was interpersonally—and professionally—dangerous. Every time he came to a decision that deviated even a little from what others wanted from him, and had come to expect from him, they heaped on the shame and guilt, and they intimated at times that his job was on the line.

It took him three years to get to where he needed to be, and everything changed about his existence. He became a far better husband and father—and a totally different minister. As he listened to himself as well as others, he felt more genuinely involved in his life. His vitality grew enormously, and his motivation soared. He could hardly contain his enthusiasm for parenting and pastoring. His wife was delighted. Perhaps best of all, he came to know himself. His contentment level inevitably skyrocketed. He began experiencing what he had preached about many times—abundant life.

■

CHRONICALLY CONTROLLED AND UNHAPPY

Last year, a brilliant woman, a forty-two-year-old wife and mother, came to me for therapy with her husband. She was discouraged with her life, and her husband was discouraged with their marriage. Things looked bad.

Jennifer came from a well-to-do, respected family. She had attended all the right schools and had a graduate degree in social work. Her father was a well-known professional, as was her husband. What's more, Jennifer had all kinds of friends, and her nine-year-old son was bright and motivated.

Nevertheless, Jennifer was deeply depressed. Her self-esteem was painfully low, and she didn't know where her life was going. All she knew was that she was chronically unhappy, that she wanted little to do with sexual intimacy, that her husband's problem with her was an irritation, and that the future looked bleak.

It didn't take me long to determine that two men were in charge of her life. She consistently gave all her power away to her dad and her husband. They did all of her choosing.

During our second session, I said, "Jennifer, I believe one reason you feel depressed and aimless is because you let other people—specifically your husband and father—determine what direction your life will take."

"I don't follow," she said.

"Well, let me put it another way. It seems that you've never taken responsibility for being the person you want to be."

She had to think about that for a while. Finally, she said, "I don't like the way that sounds, but I think you're on to something."

Jennifer and I worked together for weeks and weeks. At first, she was fearful that I would side with her husband in her struggles with him, that I would find her the "guilty one," that I would make her feel even worse about herself.

In fact, I *did* find her the guilty one, but for reasons totally different from what she expected. She was trying to do the impossible—find contentment and inner peace without living her own life. As long as she let others live her life, she was doomed to emptiness. This kind of emptiness always produces depression.

When you are depressed, as she was, your best hope is to feel your pain so intensely that your anger kicks in and you get motivated to do the work necessary to put vitality back in your life. When you get this vitality back, your life and your marriage will finally have a chance.

Though the process wasn't easy or quick, that's exactly what happened to Jennifer. She is energized and optimistic today. She has become a challenge for her husband, and she has pulled away from her stubborn, dominating father. But what a woman she has become in her own right. She is a fabulous mother, and as soon as her husband gets used to being married to a decisive, determined person, their marriage is going to be magnificent.

■

IT ALL COMES DOWN TO AUTHENTICITY

Obviously, we have a lot of ground to cover in this book. First, we need to help you get released from the frantic pursuit of momentary happiness. Then we need to help you become an authentic person. Doing this will require that you learn to be a master decision maker in every moment. Finally, as a result of this authenticity, your consciousness will inevitably be filled with a steady, deeply satisfying set of experiences that I refer to as *enduring contentment*.

I have known hundreds of persons who have had the courage to try this old-fashioned, soul-satisfying approach to contentment, and when they pursued it with all their hearts, they were inevitably successful.

I invite you to take the necessary steps for finding the most meaningful inner state available to human beings. I guarantee that if you do, your life will be filled with peace and serenity like you have never known.

part two

THE PROCESS OF
ENDURING CONTENTMENT

chapter two

OVERCOME YOUR ADDICTION
TO "HAPPINESS HIGHS"

☐An unbelievable number of Americans—as well as millions of people in other Western countries—are addicts. I'm not referring to the epidemic of drug or alcohol addiction, though we all know they are serious problems. I'm talking about an addiction to what I call *happiness highs*. Hordes of people are frantically involved in the search for immediate, rapid-fire happiness surges, and this search has become an obsession. Businesses that cater to this frenzied pursuit are flourishing. For instance, Disneyland may bill itself as "the Happiest Place on Earth," but the thrills and excitement usually wear off by the next morning or maybe by the time you find your car in the parking lot. Don't misunderstand me. I enjoy theme parks as much as anyone, but our experience at them serves as an example of the intense, short-lived happiness fix our culture seems to crave.

Every morning's newspaper is filled with promises of foolproof ways to find happiness. At least a dozen movies offer viewing experiences that are "powerful and exciting," packed with "edge-of-your-seat thrills" and "nonstop action!"

Beer commercials by the score offer to put gusto back in your life. Surely, if you down a six-pack with some pals while sitting around a campfire, you, too, can say, "It doesn't get any better than this."

Vacation spots will make your dreams come true, the Grand Deluxe LX automobile will transport you like royalty, and the latest home exercise apparatus will transform you into the person you've always wanted to be for just $39.95!

This headlong pursuit of instantaneous happiness is designed to distract us from the emptiness we feel and to numb the pain of our relational failures and our gnawing sense of futility. This addiction requires daily, sometimes hourly, fixes so there is little time or energy left to pursue healthier, more permanent solutions to our dilemmas.

Recently, one of my new clients—I'll call him Jack—told me how tired he was of the treadmill he perpetually ran on.

"Every week is essentially the same," Jack said. "I go to work each day with a nagging wish that I didn't have to. I can hardly wait for five o'clock so I can go home. I look forward to the weekends when I can watch a game on TV or head down to the mall. But I never get satisfied. My life is horribly monotonous. I sure know I'm not experiencing 'the good life,' whatever that is. My existence is not too different from mild torture."

What an incredible statement! I didn't respond immediately because I wanted the full impact of what he said to settle in. After sixty seconds of silence, Jack began to list the habits that had become deep ruts in his existence.

"When I get home at night," he began, "I get me a cold beer, and then I change into some old, comfortable clothes. I chat with my wife for a few minutes, play with the kids a little, and sit down in front of the TV. I check out the shows that are on and try to find something halfway exciting or funny. Then I grab me another beer and essentially sit in the same place until it's time to go to bed. Of course, we eat and talk some, but the beer and the television are my best hopes for a little happiness." Another long pause ensued before he added, "And the next thing I know, it's time to go to work again."

When beer and television are our best hopes for "a little happiness," for something that makes life worth living, we're in deep trouble. Obviously, many things are equivalent to Jack's "beer and television." But the paralyzing problem is this: *When we become so intent on deadening the pain and discomfort of feeling unfulfilled, there is usually no time or energy left to think about a better strategy.*

■

THE HAPPINESS ADDICTION— AND HOW IT DISTRACTS US

Never in the history of the human race has it been so easy to get a shot of momentary happiness. That's a big part of the reason so many people have become addicted to this deceptive form of internal decay. It all starts with the desire to be happy. If you become convinced that this good feeling will be the result of your interactions with the world, you'll look for every opportunity to maximize these interactions.

One form of happiness involves your being entertained by events. If you turn on the television set, surf through the channels, and eventually find a comedian, you may laugh a little. You have a few moments of fun and feel better about yourself for a short time, but that happiness soon fades. You will need the comedian to be funny again—and quickly. If not, you'll change the channel. You already need a new fix.

Another way to feed the happiness addiction is to alter your biochemistry. The most typical way is to use drugs or alcohol. Millions of people have become trapped by these chemical agents. Drugs and alcohol lead to momentary changes with disastrous long-term effects.

Happiness fixes come in all sorts of other packages. Some people try to shop themselves into a higher mood. They buy the toys that provide a momentary surge of happiness. They purchase new clothes or a new truck or new computer software. The rush that comes with acquiring things feeds the addiction.

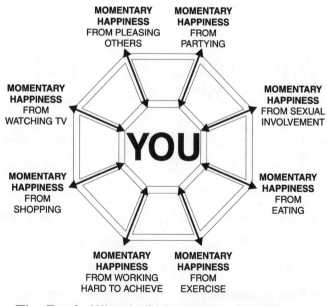

The Ferris Wheel of Momentary Happiness

One of the most insidious sources of fixes for happiness addicts is achievement. Some people nearly work themselves to death in their search for ways to get ahead. They frantically pursue the pats on the back and the esteem that come with accomplishing a goal.

However successful you are at maintaining the cycle of happiness addiction, you will never be successful enough. Here's the truth: Any gratification that comes from these actions dissolves almost immediately. The television sitcom that had you laughing a few minutes ago has no power to make you happy now. The beer you drank a little earlier has lost all its impact on you. The blouse you purchased and felt so good about this morning seems ordinary already, and you haven't even paid for it yet. You feel them, and then they're gone. You need to feel another one, and another, and another. Your pain may be numbed for a few minutes, but you can't believe how soon you have to numb it again.

This happiness-seeking habit is incredibly hard to kick. On the surface, it appears harmless enough. So what if I want to watch a little TV, then play handball, then have a few drinks? But like the person who is heavily into pornography, you always have to turn the page. The present page doesn't satisfy anymore, so you keep turning the page.

■

IMMEDIATE HAPPINESS IS *NOT* THE REAL THING

A vast majority of Americans claim that they have found a direct route to well-being. For instance, a 1996 *Los Angeles Times* poll of 1,572 respondents found that 80 percent of them were satisfied with their lives. In national surveys, a third of Americans say they are "very happy." Only one American in ten says they are "not too happy." The remainder describe themselves as "pretty happy."[1]

Sadly, at least 80 percent of all persons in virtually every sample taken in North America have professed to be more satisfied than dissatisfied. I say *sadly* because so many of these people are blinded to their predicament by the very illusion that causes people to represent themselves as "satisfied." In this "satisfied" state, they are numbed to their pain. Thinking they are "satisfied" or "happy," they focus no cognitive energy on finding new and better ways to discover deep-down contentment. They're not conscious of how desperate they are.

Amazingly, the problem appears to be worldwide. The Gallup Organization surveyed 8,787 people in more than a dozen countries. In Sweden and Canada, 95 percent of the people said they felt generally happy. Other relatively wealthy nations, such as the United States and Germany, had almost the same statistics. Even in countries with poor economies, between 60 percent and 80 percent of the population rated themselves as happy.[2]

■

HOW DO I KNOW THESE STATISTICS ARE MISLEADING?

You might be thinking, *So you're suggesting that these big polls are wrong? That all those people are in mass denial, claiming to be happy when they're not?*

Hear me out. I have two primary reasons for questioning the validity of these polls. First, an immense body of data and a huge number of psychologists, psychiatrists, and sociologists refute the claim that most people in the general population are genuinely content.

Dennis Wholey, author of *Are You Happy?*, interviewed a substantial number of national experts. The experts estimated that 20 percent of Americans are actually happy. Psychologist Archibald Hart, in his book *15 Principles for Achieving Happiness,* expressed surprise that the figure was so high. And Father John Powell, author of *Happiness Is an Inside Job*, maintains that a third of all Americans are depressed every day. He puts the number of truly happy Americans at 10 or 15 percent.

The hard statistics related to the internal emotional health of our citizens are even more alarming. William J. Bennett's 1994 *Index of Leading Cultural Indicators* includes statistics demonstrating that both physical and emotional conditions are steadily worsening for millions of Americans. In a frightening analysis of the health of our society, Bennett cites hundreds of statistics to illustrate his points. Two summary paragraphs convey the gravity of the situation:

> Over the past three decades we have experienced substantial social regression. Today the forces of social decompensation are challenging—and in some instances, overtaking—the forces of social compensation. And when decompensation takes hold, it exacts an enormous human cost. *Unless these exploding social pathologies are reversed, they will lead to the decline and perhaps even to the fall of the American republic.*
>
> During the same 30-year period there has been more than a 500 percent increase in violent crime; more than a 400 percent

increase in illegitimate births; a tripling of the percentage of children living in single-parent homes; a tripling in the teenage suicide rate; a doubling in the divorce rate; and a drop of almost 75 points in SAT scores. Modern-day social pathologies have gotten worse. They seem impervious to government spending on their alleviation, even very large amounts of spending.[3]

Here's the dilemma: In most polls, the majority of people say they're happy or satisfied with life, but hundreds of indicators prove otherwise. If people were as happy as they claim, we wouldn't have skyrocketing rates of suicide, child abuse, homicide, theft, alcoholism, and divorce. Violent crime has increased about 50 percent in the past ten years. What's more, 70 percent of all people in the United States have experienced divorce firsthand—either the divorce of their parents or their own. If present trends continue, of all the marriages that begin in the United States this year, 66 percent of them will end in separation or divorce. Five to seven million women will be beaten by someone who professes to love them. And experts fear that 10 million children will be beaten by their parents. It seems, then, that many people are saying one thing but feeling another. Otherwise, how can we explain the fundamental chaos at the center of our society?

My first reason for doubting the polls, then, is the significant body of data that gives counter evidence. My second reason for doubting the polls is the overwhelming confirmation of these unhappy statistics from my personal and professional experience. I have spent more than thirty-three years talking to all kinds of people, usually at a deep level. The vast majority of these people are searching for the elusive "something" or "someone" to enrich their lives. In most cases, a set of habits binds them, habits that they adopted in their attempt to find release and meaning.

I grant you that because I'm a clinical psychologist, many people seek me out precisely because they are dissatisfied with life. Nevertheless, a substantial proportion of my clients are high-functioning, successful people. Still, most describe themselves as "emotionally weary," "unhappy," or "depressed." Very few report that they are enduringly content.

In addition to the dozens of people who come to my office each year, I talk with hundreds of single and married persons at seminars I conduct across the country. I find the majority of singles to be frustrated with their lives and hungry for meaning and satisfaction. And while I strongly believe marriage provides the potential for deep satisfaction, most of the married persons I encounter are dissatisfied and pessimistic about their lives too.

I am convinced that the majority of Americans are severely troubled in the deepest regions of their inner lives. What most people call happiness is actually *pseudo*happiness—a counterfeit high that will quickly evaporate.

■

MOMENTARY HAPPINESS VS. ENDURING CONTENTMENT

Many people fail to differentiate between happiness and contentment—between a momentary "high" or "rush" and a deep level of satisfaction. That's because many have never experienced the kind of rich, enduring contentment we're talking about. They come to believe that all satisfaction is like cotton candy: It's sweet for a moment and dissolves an instant later. Thus, if they are to have any continuity to their good feelings, they have to pursue the sources of momentary happiness with a frenetic fervor.

It is exactly this kind of fervor that dozens of social commentators say characterizes our culture. There is no time to waste, no time for inner reflection, no time for anything internal. Turn on the television set. Shop 'til you drop. Hurry, hurry, hurry. Whatever small amount of happiness that was wrung from the last external activity is fading fast. A new fix is needed.

For instance, researcher Nora Zamichow recently explored the ramifications of a family trying to give up television. She discovered how pervasive television viewing is in America: "Television so dominates our lives that the average U.S. household has a set turned on for seven hours each day. Two-thirds of us watch television while eating dinner and more than half of 4- to 6-year-olds would rather watch TV than spend time with dads, studies show."[4]

I suspect that television viewing is one of America's most damaging addictions. It may well get in the way of the pursuit of authenticity more often than any other habit.

■

CONTENTMENT IS ACHIEVED IN A DIFFERENT WAY

In contrast to the frantic pursuit of happiness fixes, enduring contentment is realized in a far more peaceful way. It requires considerably more courage, but there is nothing frenzied or hysterical about the process of achieving it. Rather, it is more a matter of sitting back and being patient, of moving inside oneself and exploring one's inner terrain.

As I stated earlier, contentment is almost always the result of a person becoming authentic, becoming the person he or she really is. This involves a lot of "inside" work, a lot of reflection time. This is why addiction to TV and radio, compulsive shopping, incessant overwork, and all the characteristics of our fast-moving culture often sabotage our efforts to discover how to live a contented life. *As long as we are focused outside ourselves, our pursuit of authenticity is sure to be futile and disappointing.*

When you aren't living your life authentically, you are likely to be in terrible pain. You may not be consciously aware of this pain, but it will darken your days nonetheless. In the midst of this pain, you have three choices:

1. You can seek enough "happiness surges" to distract you from this emptiness at the center of yourself.
2. You can look for pain deadeners, something that will numb your consciousness twenty-four hours a day.
3. You can search within yourself for a way to become authentic.

Unfortunately, most people pursue these alternatives in exactly this order. They play the superficial games that are sold by our society—be more, do more, get more, experience more. Then when they realize, sometimes after years or decades, that these pursuits are ultimately unsatisfying, they try to deaden the pain. If the pain deadeners they utilize are insufficient—and hopefully they will be—people may try alternative number three. This is when they have a chance to be "regenerated," to grow and develop in new ways, to rediscover their soul, to find that self they truly are. Then the excitement of their life begins to build within them.

■

ACTION PLAN FOR OVERCOMING THE ADDICTION TO HAPPINESS HIGHS

Deep-down, soul-satisfying contentment can never be realized until you recognize and overcome your addiction to happiness highs. The eradication of this addiction requires that you take a courageous stand, and you have to expect a fierce battle. Here's a five-step action plan designed to help you break the habit of squandering your life in the pursuit of happiness surges:

1. Take inventory. This step requires a long look at your life.

- How contented are you deep within yourself?
- If your schedule is frantic, how gratifying are the payoffs?
- Do you experience plenty of peace and serenity?
- Or do you feel a chronic need to do more, to fill your days with a torrent of activity and stimulation?

After you've taken this inventory, you may wish to rate your level of inner contentment.

Level of Inner Contentment

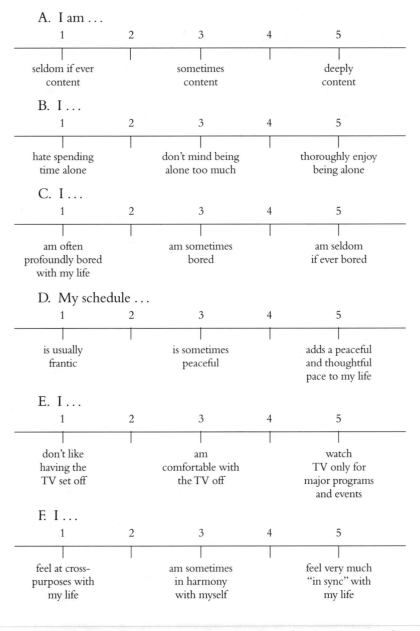

A. I am . . .

1	2	3	4	5
seldom if ever content		sometimes content		deeply content

B. I . . .

1	2	3	4	5
hate spending time alone		don't mind being alone too much		thoroughly enjoy being alone

C. I . . .

1	2	3	4	5
am often profoundly bored with my life		am sometimes bored		am seldom if ever bored

D. My schedule . . .

1	2	3	4	5
is usually frantic		is sometimes peaceful		adds a peaceful and thoughtful pace to my life

E. I . . .

1	2	3	4	5
don't like having the TV set off		am comfortable with the TV off		watch TV only for major programs and events

F. I . . .

1	2	3	4	5
feel at cross-purposes with my life		am sometimes in harmony with myself		feel very much "in sync" with my life

Score: For each statement, anything less than a five shows an area of your life where contentment is lacking some or all of the time.

One of my closest friends, a fellow psychologist, took this kind of inventory a few months ago after his wife moved out for the second time. His pain was excruciating, and that's why he finally looked at his life. He discovered weekdays that were far too long and intense and weekends that were filled with racquetball, golf, conferences, and trips. Late nights and early mornings characterized his sleep patterns. A treadmill of activity kept him constantly on the move. His wife's leaving was the result of his addictive pursuit of happiness highs that made the attainment of true contentment virtually impossible. This difficult inventory was the first step on the road to recovery for my friend.

2. *Experience your pain.* You'll never kick your addiction to happiness surges until the pain that results from pursuing them is so intense that you decide to do something about it. If your life is constantly stressful, if your schedule is overly full or out of control, if you regularly feel on the verge of emptiness, let this stress, franticness, and boredom register clearly in your brain. If your hunger for serenity hasn't been satisfied for a long time and you're famished, take a long look at how this feels. Habits turn into addictions when they become so routine that they are like breathing. To break deeply ingrained habits, you must be highly motivated. This motivation grows out of the pain you feel in pursuit of whatever you are addicted to. The difficult part of kicking the habit of pursuing happiness highs is that you may hide from the pain or push it out of your mind. Then you return to the same old behaviors—totally unaware that pain will one more time tighten its strangling grip on you.

I recommended to my psychologist friend that he write out his feelings of pain on a sheet of paper and read what he had written at least three times a week for six weeks. His success at breaking this addiction depended on staying in touch with his pain, and there is only one way to keep your pain in view—continue looking at it and recognizing it for what it is.

3. Surround yourself with people who will support you and hold you accountable. Find at least two or three persons who have recognized the perils of pursuing happiness highs—and who are well along in breaking this hard-to-see but destructive habit. When these allies share their insights and encouragement, you'll have the support you need to make strides forward.

If you have no friends who can do this, here are some other ways you can get the support you need:

- Join a therapy group.
- Start a group yourself at your work or church.
- Attend meetings at your church or synagogue.

4. Identify the sources of your happiness highs and deal with them directly. If you spend endless hours in front of the TV, unplug your set—or get rid of it altogether. If your addiction is shopping, avoid malls and your favorite stores with all your might. If you're accustomed to working long hours, force yourself to leave the office at a reasonable hour and reserve your weekends for leisure time.

5. Set aside consistent times to be alone, to think and reflect, to become familiar with your inner world. You must understand why you're drawn toward short-term happiness surges and become aware of your thoughts and emotions, which will enable you to pursue true contentment. (We'll discuss this process at length in the next chapter.)

This plan is designed to help you end an addiction that is sure to lead to dire results if you don't deal with it decisively. Without action, you could become totally blind to your frantic process. Your chronic lack of contentment risks the deterioration of your primary functioning in your marriage, career, friendships, and spiritual growth. If you stay too long with an inner state that lacks contentment, you set yourself up for significant personal loss. Surges of happiness may bring temporary rushes, but they will leave you desperately wanting in the end. And they will require more and more of your energy to replenish their rapidly evaporating rewards.

■

ONE MAN'S FRANTIC SEARCH TO BUY CONTENTMENT

Sometimes the journey from addiction to authenticity is frighteningly long and perilous. I worked for years with a man I'll call Glen. He tried with all his heart, strength, and mind to buy the good life. The youngest of four children, Glen was brought up in Southern California in a lower-middle-class family that struggled every month to make ends meet. Glen's dad worked in an automobile assembly plant, and his mother worked part-time in a dry cleaning shop down the street from their home.

Money became important for the family only when there wasn't enough—a situation that became more and more frequent as Glen got older. With two of his siblings in college and the other one in need of constant medical care, money was *the* issue for Glen's family all through his junior and senior high school years. The lack of money produced so much stress that the family lost their ability to have fun and enjoy one another. Glen's sense of importance got trampled in the chase to pay the monthly bills.

Glen graduated from high school with a reasonably good grade point average, attended two years of junior college while he worked nights at a grocery store, and met Stacy, the girl he eventually married. Along with all of the normal adjustments attendant to a new marriage, this young couple had to deal with Glen's obsessive need to become financially secure. He worked two jobs, he insisted that his wife work, and he bought an old house to fix up for resale. That was during the early stages of a real estate boom in California, and Glen parlayed the profit from his refurbished house into a bigger house with an adjoining duplex. His upward financial progress was little short of spectacular.

With a tidy savings account and income from the rental of the duplex, Glen quit one of his jobs and let his wife quit hers. But there was no letup in the frantic pursuit of money, material things, and financial security. He tried to slow down from time to time, but the money that was scarce during his growing-up years seemed so readily available now that he couldn't resist grabbing more. Before long, he started a real estate investment company, secured some shrewd partners, and amassed a large collection of holdings. Every time Glen closed a big deal, he enjoyed a rush of adrenaline. But when the thrill wore off, he hurried on to his next moneymaking venture.

Glen and Stacy had two children along the way—children he wanted to love and immerse himself in. But by then he was buying apartment buildings in Texas and Arizona, and he was seldom home with his family.

Within ten years, he built a giant operation, made millions, bought four homes and numerous cars, and gave his kids every financial opportunity—but he attended to virtually nothing in his personal life. His marriage was built almost exclusively on living the "big life"—fancy cars, Caribbean vacations, and courtside season tickets to the Laker games. And his kids came to expect all the luxuries and comforts money could buy.

■

PSEUDOHAPPINESS IS DISTURBINGLY FLEETING

By the time Glen came to my office, the real estate market was plummeting as wildly as it had soared ten years earlier. Desperately hoping the economy would level out, he had tried to hold on to his empire. In the middle of his financial crisis, another problem began to surface—his emotional turmoil.

Glen told me that Stacy, whom he had kept out of his finances through the good years, didn't understand his predicament now. She neither offered empathy during his sleepless nights nor stopped spending at the same reckless pace she had become accustomed to. She was turned off by Glen's gloominess, irritated by his pessimism, and shocked by his neediness. They hadn't made love for several weeks—and only then when he virtually demanded it. Their relationship, which had run on autopilot for years, was empty and lifeless.

Glen's addiction to happiness surges was so blatant that it was impossible not to see that it would eventually leave him feeling hollow. He had tried one of society's "guaranteed" strategies—accumulate enough money to bankroll a glamorous, glitzy lifestyle. He was sure that would make him feel good about himself and secure all the deep contentment for which he longed. Fortunately for him, he found out soon enough that this wouldn't work.

During the months I worked with Glen, I walked him through the five steps I outlined earlier. When he stopped dashing from one happiness surge to the next, his schedule opened up enough for him to examine himself. Glen rediscovered his internal world. I eventually worked with the entire family. In time, he and his wife and their children developed healthy patterns, and they gave up their old ways. They essentially began to discover a deeper and more substantive part of their authentic selves.

I cannot even begin to tell you how delighted they are today—delighted not because they had to go through all that pain, of course, but because they discovered the way to contentment before it was too late.

■

EMOTIONAL HEALTH AND AUTHENTICITY

Kicking the addiction to happiness highs—and taking the first steps toward authenticity—demands a total commitment to emotional health. I have never known an authentic person who was not emotionally healthy. However, I have known hundreds of people who purported to be "happy" but who severely lacked emotional health and authenticity.

If you have enough money, good looks, brains, or charisma, you can obtain some short-term happiness. But it won't last.

If you know down deep that your life is currently filled with momentary, rapidly fading pseudohappiness, that you really aren't authentic in your present condition, I promise you that you have a lot to gain from reading the rest of this book. In the following chapters, I will describe to you all of the insights I've gained through years of working with thousands of people at deep levels. I've watched men and women turn dull, miserable, unsatisfying lives into energy-filled, joyful, exciting, authentic, and loving lives.

I wish for you a rich and deeply meaningful sense of contentment at the center of your being. There is no good reason why you can't obtain it.

■

chapter three

LOOK INWARD

Some life events are so powerful that they are indelibly branded into our consciousness, even if we are not directly involved in them. For instance, I often think about an incident that occurred more than twenty years ago when our family lived in Chicago.

On a Saturday morning, our neighbor was mowing his front lawn. His three-year-old boy, Jimmy, was riding his tricycle on the sidewalk. Jimmy fell and hit his knee on the concrete and began to cry. Two bigger boys—five and six years old—laughed at Jimmy from across the street because he cried.

Jimmy's dad, who may have felt some insecurity about his son's lack of toughness, immediately stopped his work and snapped, "Jimmy! Get up from there, and stop that crying! You're not hurt!"

Jimmy eventually stopped crying, but I've always wondered what was going on inside his head. I've sometimes imagined that he was thinking to himself, *Boy, for a minute there I thought I really was hurt!*

Through the years, I heard Jimmy's dad yell the same basic message to him hundreds of times: "Get up from there, and stop that crying! You're not hurt!" From an early age, Jimmy learned that he should ignore feelings of fragility and vulnerability.

It isn't just the little Jimmys who have been told to disregard their internal messages. The same is often true for little Kathys. The reasons may be different, but the result is almost always the same. While little boys are told to "be tough" and "act like a big boy," little girls are told to be sweet, proper, and nice. Kathy's parents may feel threatened or uncomfortable if she shows any aggressive feelings or anything hinting at anger or sexuality. She is told—verbally or nonverbally—"good girls don't behave that way." So she pretends she doesn't have such feelings or thoughts.

And when Jimmy and Kathy regularly hear that they should quit thinking or feeling something their parents don't want them to think or feel, it isn't long until they start ignoring their internal data altogether. Soon they are completely oblivious to the messages sounding within them.

■

JIMMY AND KATHY GROW UP EMOTIONALLY DISABLED

Since enduring contentment requires living authentically, any person who is cut off from internal information is bound to be discontent. You cannot be authentic if you have shut down vital inner messages that contribute to understanding yourself.

Please don't jump to false conclusions. I do not believe our feelings, thoughts, and wishes should exclusively dictate our decisions and actions. We all know people who are perpetually wrung out emotionally, always seem to be in crisis, and make terrible decisions based on selfish whims and impulses. It's likely that these people have not learned to *balance* their internal messages with data that come from sources external to them. It's unhealthy and unwise to base all of our decisions on internal information alone.

Having issued this caveat, I must say that the majority of people in North America today suffer the opposite problem. They are so distant from their internal world that their decision making is severely disabled. When this happens, the chance of becoming authentic is slim. They are totally unprepared to make good choices and decisions moment by moment. And inevitably they will surrender their decision-making responsibilities to other people or groups of people. At this point, they are on a fast path to becoming totally lost.

Consider that young boy, Jimmy. Let's assume that he is twenty-five years old today, newly married, and in the early stages of starting a family of his own. Given his dad's frequent demands for him to disregard his internal messages, Jimmy is likely to be a stranger to his inner world. And given that he is a stranger to this most intimate part of himself, he is miserably ill-equipped to act wisely in relation to his wife, children, friends, employers, and others.

If Jimmy doesn't know what he really feels or thinks, how can he represent himself accurately? He can't be true to who he is because he doesn't *know* who he is. He has become disconnected from those internal messages that would make his feelings and thoughts available at each moment.

In this state of deprivation, he is not prepared to contribute anything unique or helpful to the communication with his wife, the development of his children, or the relationships with his friends. He acts on assumptions and suppositions. Since other people his age think one way, he assumes he must think the same way. Or since his dad related to his children in a certain way, Jimmy supposes he should follow suit.

Under these conditions, he is a prime candidate for chronic emptiness, dissatisfaction, and sadness. It all starts with shutting down the messages from deep within.

■

TWO REASONS WE MUST LOOK INWARD

Authenticity involves the relentless determination and ability to make one good decision after another, and *good decision making is an internal event for every person on earth.* This is why I am so concerned about people who have never become comfortable with exploring their inner world.

When you fail to explore and embrace your inner world, you are almost sure to mismanage two parts of the decision-making process. First, if you fail to look inward you won't take possession of any internal data—your thoughts, feelings, needs, wishes, and concerns. Clearly, this will jeopardize any decision you eventually make. You won't know what *you* feel about the matter at hand. You will have to rely on what other people tell you.

Second, and even more important, if you fail to look inward and don't listen closely to yourself, you are in no position to deal with your thoughts, others' thoughts, and your values, and you will be unable to stand in the middle of all this information and make a solid decision.

Persons who have never learned to feel comfortable in their internal world become hamstrung in managing their lives. They may sell out and give over their personhood to some influential person or group of persons. If they finally give these "choosing rights" over to someone else, a tragic personal event occurs. It is as though they commit emotional suicide. They give up on being who they truly are.

■

THE PREDICAMENT MAY START AT AN EARLY DEVELOPMENTAL AGE

All of us are fundamentally motivated by an intense desire to feel good about ourselves. This seems to be an inherent part of our nature. Most of us have wanted to feel good about ourselves since we were old enough to feel, and that was even before we began storing these feelings in memory banks in our brains. Early in my career as a psychologist, I came to believe that the desire to feel good about ourselves is the most powerful motivational force that propels and directs us.

In fact, we may have started trying to feel good about ourselves around the time we began to encounter our *self* in our first year of life— a self we recognized as "me." We began to distinguish the difference between feeling "good" and feeling "not good." And even as infants, we may have begun to make basic choices that distanced ourselves from our internal messages.

Let me explain: Evidence shows that an infant alters his crying in response to cues given by his mother, cues that are transmitted through the mother's body language—her facial expression, her tone of voice, the tension or relaxation of her muscles. If the baby—we'll call him Joey—was crying when the mother picked him up, and if the mother was tense and cold, the baby distinguishes this from a more relaxed and warm touch. If the baby links these two messages—crying brings a cold, stiff response while not crying brings a warm, nurturing response—he may very well quiet down. (I'm not saying a baby reasons all this out, of course. All of these subtle messages are received subconsciously.)

Under these circumstances, Joey is faced with an insoluble dilemma. He must choose between his internal message ("This diaper is hurting me, so I'll cry") and the external considerations ("If I shut up, Mom will cuddle me and coo over me"). But which stimulus package does Joey heed? If he opts to respond to his mother's desires and wishes while denying his needs and feelings, he may begin a pattern of ignoring his internal messages. But if he denies the clear messages from his mother, he may experience some loss in his relationship with this significant person. In a sense, he is in a no-win situation. This is the same predicament he will face—in many different forms—as long as he lives. And herein exists the makings of what I call "out-of-syncness."

You may know from experience what I mean by out-of-syncness. It refers to the inner sense of disharmony, of being different in word and deed from what you are feeling. When you feel out of sync, you almost always have failed to give adequate attention to an important part of your internal data. When that part is unrepresented, it is like your internal engine misfires. You become a four-cylinder vehicle trying to operate on two cylinders. Conversely, you are in sync when you feel totally unified within yourself, as if you are presenting exactly the same self you truly are at your depths.

Whether Joey values his mother's happiness as the most powerful and direct way to produce good feelings about himself or assumes that paying close attention to his internal stimuli will most effectively bring about a satisfying inner state, you can be sure of one thing: On some level of his increasingly complex neurological system, there will come a decision about how to play this out. And this decision will revolve around his already pressing need to feel good about himself.

If Joey opts to please his mother, to respond sacrificially to her indications of discomfort, and if his mother responds with a happy face and nurturing sounds to Joey's cessation of crying, there will be the automatic good feelings that nearly always come from pleasing the important other. He will, momentarily, feel good about himself.

Whatever happened to the discomfort of the diaper? The little inner voice may have been heard on the neurological loudspeaker system: "Don't pay attention to your body or your feelings. What's important now is what your mother wants from you." To whatever degree this becomes a pattern for Joey, to this same degree he is bound to lose touch with himself.

As the years pass, such choices become far more clear and significant. In junior high school, Joey's friends want him to pass them the answers to the history test. But something inside tells him that's wrong. What should he do? Disregard his inner urging not to cheat or risk rejection from his peers? And when the time comes to select a college, Joey wants to attend the University of Southern California, which has a strong film program, but Dad insists he go to Duke—to "carry on the family tradition." Whom should he please? Then years later, when Joe's boss pressures him to work Saturday, the same day as his son's Little League championship game, Joe again feels that tension: *My gut tells me I have to be at Joe Jr.'s game, but I'm in line for that promotion. What should I do?*

You see my point. The dilemma that begins early on—weighing one's inner messages against the needs and wishes of others—continues throughout life. And how we respond to such choices is critical to our pursuit of true contentment. We may not have been able to control the early influences in our lives, but even if we have developed a pattern of neglecting our internal messages, we can later retrain ourselves to respect and heed them.

■

THE CHALLENGE THAT SURPASSES ALL OTHERS

Whether you are raising a young child or trying to develop a higher degree of authenticity in your own life, the most important struggle of all involves maintaining a healthy balance of attentiveness to both internal and external information sources. If you neglect either source, your authenticity will suffer.

For several months, I counseled Steve, a thirty-two-year-old man who placed far too much weight on his parents' input. He seldom paid much attention to his own thoughts, feelings, needs, and desires. At our first session, Steve told me he was extremely lonely because he had no intimate relationships. He wanted to get married but was hesitant because his parents "needed him."

"I couldn't just abandon my parents like that," he told me. "I mean, what would they do if I got married?"

"I assume they'd continue on with their lives," I said. "You told me they're active and in relatively good health—"

"That's true," he broke in, "but they still rely on me to help them a lot around their house—you know, fixing things, moving furniture. Besides, I've dated girls before, and I even took one girlfriend, Shelly, home to meet my parents. Mom and Dad didn't think she was right for me."

"But what did you think?"

"Well, my folks told me that—"

"Right, but what did *you* think about Shelly?"

He sat for a while without saying a word. "I thought she was really nice and everything, but my parents said she was unambitious."

"Listen, Steve, it's fine that you want to help your parents and listen to their opinions—to a point. It's critical that you learn to listen to yourself, to attend to your own needs."

He was ready with another counterpunch.

"Yeah, but my folks have been married thirty-seven years. They know what it takes to make a relationship successful."

Week after week, I tried different strategies to help Steve move inside himself and give his thoughts and convictions the credit they deserved, but he wouldn't have it. He had a bag full of excuses and rationales for why he should listen to everyone—especially his parents—

53

except himself. My guess is that he will never marry unless he overcomes his entrenched pattern of disregarding his intrinsic prompting. He gives too much credence to what other people think, and he is too ambivalent about his needs and inclinations.

If Steve was extreme in his inability to embrace his inner world, there are others who fall on the opposite end of the spectrum. These people are far too centered on their own thoughts and feelings. They show no signs of even caring what the important people in their life feel and need. And this imbalance can be just as unhealthy as Steve's.

All this is to say that one of the fundamental challenges of being human is learning to live your life so that you are in sync with yourself *and* all the crucial people in your world. That is, it's vital to be true to yourself *and* your friends, parents, spouse, and others at the same time. Doing this is not easy, but it's certainly possible. And enduring contentment is a natural consequence if you can master this skill.

■

FIVE WAYS TO KNOW YOURSELF BETTER

I've tried my best to convince you that paying attention to your internal world is vital to your attainment of soul-satisfying contentment. Now I want to give you a plan for increasing your internal awareness. Here are five specific suggestions for achieving greater internal awareness. Give this project careful consideration.

1. Write out your intention. On a piece of paper or an index card, write what you hope to accomplish—and how you're going to accomplish it—and post it on your refrigerator or bathroom mirror or anywhere you're sure to see it every day. Your message might be as simple as this one:

- I want to know myself incredibly well.
- I want to become fully aware of all my deepest thoughts and feelings.
- I want to listen long and hard to the flow of vital information that is constantly available within me.
- So here's what I plan to do. I will spend at least thirty minutes alone every day—thinking and journaling. I will also find a friend with whom I can sort through all that I'm thinking and feeling.

Having your goal and plan of action clearly outlined will keep you on track and moving forward.

2. Write in a journal or notebook every day. You don't need to write for more than ten or fifteen minutes, but it's critical that you write your honest thoughts and feelings as they come to you. The goal is to practice tapping in to your internal reservoir. The more you do this, the more naturally the journaling will come to you.

3. Read something every day that stimulates your internal process. For example, I read a chapter from the Bible each morning. I especially find the writings of the apostle Paul beneficial.

This kind of reading has a way of leading you toward the center of yourself. If you read with a personal perspective—that is, how the writing affects you and speaks to your daily needs—you will get more deeply in touch with your inner thoughts and feelings.

4. Spend regular time with people who know themselves well and who encourage you to talk about what you feel most strongly. Get personal with these people. Try to understand them as best you can, and tell them as fully as possible about who you are.

5. Pray. Prayer is meant to be a conversation with God. It involves pouring out your heart to Him about what is most on your mind and then listening intently to what He says to you in response. I try to do this every day, and I can tell you that prayer has had more influence on my life and my work with people than anything else I do.

■

TAKE A LESSON FROM ONE WHO KNOWS HER INNER WORLD

I know an eighty-four-year-old woman named Vivian. She is sublimely content. Hers is a quiet, self-assured satisfaction that is almost palpable to those around her. If she were asked to rate her sense of well-being, she would say it is extremely high.

If you met her, she would treat you gently and with great dignity. She would immediately mention something she liked about you. "What a delightful smile you have," she might say. Or, "Oh, you're studying to be a veterinarian. That's a wonderful choice." You would quickly sense that she found you interesting and worthy of respect.

If you raised any question for her, she would take it on. She would make sure she knew exactly what you were asking, and then she would look off into the distance and puzzle over what she thought and felt about your question. You could almost see her checking her internal data! Eventually, her answer would come. It would be precisely "the truth" for Vivian. She might make several statements such as "I don't know for sure, but it seems to me…" or "Here's the way it strikes me, but see what you think…."

And if you disagreed with Vivian, she would want to investigate with you your reasons—because she might want to change her opinion if she thought you were right. And if you scolded her because you thought she was dead wrong, she would try to calm you down a little so she could do some more exploring with you. Her self-worth does not depend in the slightest on being right or having you agree with her. She only pursues to the best of her ability what she senses to be the truth.

I know Vivian unusually well, and I have since I was a boy in junior high school. She was the maid and nanny for a family whose son I grew up with. She has not had an easy life, but she has experienced soul-satisfying contentment like few people I know have achieved. Her secret is that she knows her inner world like most of us know our own homes. She freely assimilates and assesses all this information and makes one solid choice after another. And all the time she is choosing and deciding, she treats you in the same gentle, loving, respectful way that she treats herself.

Clearly, Vivian is totally in sync with herself. She is who she is, and she feels good about herself. She has become a person who can be joyful in her suffering, happy in good times and bad. Nothing that could ever happen to her would compromise her sense of life satisfaction. Addictions of various kinds to shortcut contentment are unthinkable to her. She doesn't hunger for more money, more recognition, or more of anything. She is glad to be alive and will be until the day she dies. She is magnificently *authentic!*

All of us long for the rich contentment that Vivian exemplifies. It all begins way down at the center of you in your inner world. To the degree that you can stay solidly in touch with your internal messages, deeply aware of all your data—especially your thoughts, feelings, needs, and wishes—then you are well on your way to experiencing contentment.

chapter four

■

CONSCIOUSLY PROCESS EVERY
DECISION YOU MAKE

☐Individuals who strive to attain a deep sense of inner satisfaction will be bombarded with suggestions about how to go about it. People, institutions, and society in general will offer innumerable tactics for procuring peace of mind and happiness. Whether simple or complex, each of these strategies promises a potent payoff.

Many formulas for happiness cater to a quick-fix mentality. Drink a beer or two, and feel the rapid reduction of your anxiety. Buy a new outfit, and feel your mood rise as you envision how good you're going to look. Indulge in a cruise, and you'll feel pampered and special.

Other strategies promise long-term satisfaction. If you put in countless hours at your job, you may get a promotion, a big bonus, increased status, or a handsome raise—which may lead to a new home in a more exclusive area, with added admiration from your friends and peers. If you toil unflaggingly so that you can become a partner someday, work weekends for a possible promotion, or labor at two jobs to bolster your savings account, you are sure to feel so much better about yourself eventually—partially because others will feel so much better about you.

Strategy after strategy is designed to help you feel better about yourself. Try to fulfill the expectations of your parents, your kids, your spouse, your boss, your neighbors, or any other important person. Figure out what they want from you, and then strive to give them whatever it is. Become a doctor because Mom and Dad would be so proud—even though you hate science. Join a certain church because your best friend thinks it would be good for you—even though you much prefer the church across town. Take the promotion that comes with a handsome raise but requires travel every other weekend—even though you would much rather be home with your children.

It doesn't matter that all these people want something from you that requires you to be inauthentic, to jettison your deeply held wishes and predilections. All you have to do is please them, and their increasingly good feelings about you will help you feel better about yourself. The problem is, in the end you won't be one step closer to true contentment.

It's not so much that living your life to satisfy external criteria is wrong in itself. What other people want from you is an important consideration, but when you overlook or seriously discount your internal needs, thoughts, and feelings, your contentment level is almost sure to be jeopardized.

.

THERE IS NO SUBSTITUTE FOR IN-SYNCNESS

If strategies for finding contentment do not come from within you, they won't work for long. In fact, you can develop yourself into anything you want, accumulate incredible wealth, garner enormous status, and become as well liked by your parents and everyone else as one could be, but your good feeling will be fleeting if you are not in harmony with all of your thoughts, emotions, and desires.

When I talk with people who are passionately pursuing a strategy to gain contentment, I know almost immediately if the effort is going to succeed or not. How do I know? I listen. *Obsession about their goal or an irrational drive fueling their pursuit of it is a dead giveaway of eventual failure.* Even more important, I check to see if they are listening to themselves. If they are no longer in contact with their deepest thoughts and feelings, they're almost certainly not in sync. And once they are out of sync, any happiness they derive from their efforts will not have depth or staying power. It will naturally die away, and disillusionment will take its place.

The story of in-syncness all starts with that baby we discussed in the last chapter—the baby who had to choose between attending to his own discomfort or his mother's. Before we return to the baby, however, we need to examine how we want the baby to end up.

■

OPERATING OUT OF YOUR CONTROL BOOTH

I want to develop a picture for you that has grown out of thousands and thousands of conversations I've had with individuals hungry to feel good about themselves. Imagine that at the center of your brain there is a control booth. It is a round room with glass windows encircling it. Available to you in this room are several phones, fax machines, satellite hookups, state-of-the-art computers, Internet access, and tele-conferencing equipment. Your challenge, while standing at the center of this room, is to make good choices from moment to moment that will determine how you move through life.

To make these choices effectively, you will need open communication lines between you in your control booth and all the important data sources in your life. These sources include:

1. All your feelings and all your relevant thoughts, all the wisdom you have gleaned from past successes and failures (*internal*).
2. The feedback from significant people in your life, information about important cultural guidelines, and facts from experts (*external*).
3. Direction based on your spiritual faith and convictions (*values*).

Once you have fully informed yourself on the basis of input from each data source, your assignment is to stand in the middle of all this information and make the best possible choice about the issue at hand. If you make one decision after another based on full and complete data, and if you do so thoughtfully and skillfully, you will end up being in sync with yourself. But if you make choices without consulting all the data sources—perhaps listening to only one source—you will inevitably make decisions that will render you out of sync or inauthentic. If this happens, whatever happiness you experience will be fragile and short-lived.

Several of my clients and friends employ this decision-making model. When they need to make a decision, they literally imagine themselves going into their control booth, shutting the door and locking it, and beginning the process of data collection and evaluation.

Recently, one of my clients, a lawyer I'll call Walter, described an experience from the previous week.

"I was in court," he said, "and during a vehement argument with the other counsel, the judge suddenly interrupted and asked both of us to join him in his private chambers. I didn't have the slightest idea what was up. When he closed the door, he said he would entertain a motion for a new trial. He gave his reasons and asked the other lawyer and me to comment. It was a poignant moment, and I needed to make just the right response."

Walter and I had worked for several months on his decision-making process, especially when he was under intense stress. He had a history of making impulsive choices that he regretted a few hours after he made them.

"I immediately remembered what we have worked on," Walter continued. "I went into my control booth, closed and locked the door, and I began to collect all the vital information. I let the other lawyer talk first so I could have more time. Once I got all the available data, I sifted through it and practiced two or three decisions. I eventually chose one of them. And when I finally spoke, I said exactly what I wanted to say."

At that point, Walter's face broke into a broad grin.

"The judge seemed taken with my approach, and in time he went along with me. There will be no new trial. From my point of view, it made no sense at all. And the judge agreed."

Walter had practiced the kind of decision making that is at the heart of authenticity. He was ecstatic about his ability to know his inner world and to express himself in a genuine and persuasive way.

■

IT STARTS WITH DATA COLLECTION

If you want to be in sync with the deepest and most important parts of yourself, begin with data collection. As fully and objectively as possible, gather all important information from every available source.

Still, even when you deliberately and conscientiously cull data from all your sources, seldom will any decision be simple and straightforward. Almost every choice will involve conflicting information from your various sources. Many of your data sources will give you mixed signals about how you can most effectively get the job done. You will have to say no to several sources in order to say yes to others.

Suppose a young single mother named Kim is planning to go out on a special date but is suddenly shocked by a four o'clock call from her ill baby-sitter, who is forced to cancel. Now she has no one to watch her two children, and her date, Kurt, is supposed to pick her up in two hours. Kim has a crucial decision to make. Input and information would come from several places:

- Her own feelings: "How much do I want to go on this date, and how hard am I willing to work to make it happen?"
- The desires of her children: "We don't want a new baby-sitter, Mommy. The last one you had stay with us was weird!"

- Kurt's wishes: "This is important to me. I've been planning this evening for weeks, and I really want us to go."
- Her value-driven thoughts: "My kids come first, but Kurt is a great guy, and he deserves for me to at least try to work this out."
- The voice of her mother: "I had no social life when you were young because I wanted to always be there for you. It was a sacrifice, of course, but it's what a mother should do."
- The words of her neighbor: "If you ever need help with the kids, give me a call."

To stay in sync with herself, this young mother must process information from all these sources. Fortunately for her, she has a brain, like you and I do, with the capacity to assimilate and evaluate massive amounts of data. In order to make a wise decision that was true to herself, Kim needed to listen to all of this input and weigh it carefully. If she gave one source too much weight or ignored it altogether, she may have made a poor choice that was not in sync with her inner world. She eventually decided to call her neighbor, to "interview" her, and to prevail on her for the help she needed. Everyone ended up winning.

■

DATA COLLECTION CAN TAKE AN INSTANT OR YEARS

Kim had two hours to decide whether to keep her date or cancel it. Other decisions must be made faster than that—sometimes instantaneously. A friend asks how you like her new outfit. In the span of two or three seconds, you must formulate a response. A coworker asks you out on a date. Do you say yes, no, or perhaps another time? In a staff meeting, your boss asks if you agree with the strategy for the new product line. He wants an answer *now*. Two components aid you in times like this: (1) your brain, which can analyze extensive information in a nanosecond, and (2) practice. As you hone data-collection skills, the process becomes more fluid and natural. You can quickly access your input sources and make a reliable split-second decision.

Most often, the bigger the decision, the more time is required to make it. Much of my work is done with couples who are thinking about getting married. This monumental decision—which I hope will happen only once in a lifetime for them—is so crucial to the well-being of these two people that they need to be absolutely sure they are in sync with themselves.

Since research indicates that dating for at least two years ensures the best chance for a successful marriage,[5] couples would be wise to spend plenty of time gathering data. They must analyze their emotions, talk with friends and family members, read books about marriage, take personality tests, and discuss every conceivable topic together. Ample time must be allowed to do a thorough investigation.

I've discovered that with matters both large and small, almost no one ever complains about having collected *too much* data. But many people lament, "Why was I in such a hurry to get married?" Or, "I should have thought more about leaving my old job—my new one is a drag." Impatience and impulsiveness are enemies of good decision making. Acquiesce to either one, and you jeopardize the final decision and your overall sense of being in sync with yourself.

One precaution on this point: Don't use the data-collection process as an excuse to continually delay making a decision. Some people are so afraid of making a bad choice that they become stuck. From time to time, a couple who have been dating for two or three years will come to my office for therapy. What prompts their visit is a conflict over whether or not to get married. Specifically, one of the partners—usually the man—is reluctant to make the leap.

"When it comes to marriage," I'll say to the anxious fellow, "it's extremely wise to take your time and make sure you know everything you can about yourself and your partner. So do you feel like you have all the information necessary to make a prudent choice?"

"Well, I guess so," he'll say.

"No, no. Don't guess. This is too important."

"All right then, yes. We've dated for two and a half years. We've discussed every topic we can think of. We've seen each other in lots of situations. What else?"

"That's what I was going to ask you. It sounds like it's time to evaluate everything you've learned and come to a conclusion."

At this point, he is usually shifting in his chair and looking at his feet, while his girlfriend sits forward, wearing a smug grin. I'm certainly not trying to railroad this guy, and I surely don't want him to become rattled and make a poor choice. But the truth is, if he knows everything he needs to know, it's time to decide. Procrastination and indecision won't help him or his girlfriend.

Whether the issue is getting married, choosing a career, or deciding whether to go back to school, allow as much time as you need to assemble data—and then act.

■

EVERYONE MUST BE TAUGHT DECISION-MAKING SKILLS

People who want to experience deep-down contentment must be in sync with themselves—with the deepest and most profound parts of themselves. To be in sync with themselves, they must occupy their control booth and have input available from every possible information source. And they must *know how* to make decisions based on the data that will ensure growth and development. This last point must be given a great deal of attention if they are to experience contentment.

Children are not born with good decision-making ability; it has to be taught to them. Without question, this is the single most important skill they will ever learn. Any parent who wants to set up a child for a lifetime of satisfaction and meaning will carefully attend to this vital component of maturity. The following outline illustrates how a parent can help a child master the decision-making process:

1. The parent carefully assists the child in collecting all his or her internal data (feelings, thoughts, goals) and crucial external data (parent's desires or perhaps a friend's feelings). The parent does this by employing a mixture of listening, questioning, and repeating back to the child.

2. The parent thinks with the child about the decision that needs to be made in light of all this information. As much as possible, the parent lets the child take the lead—just as though he or she were learning to walk—offering guidance and assistance only when necessary.

3. The parent assumes the role of boundary setter and boundary enforcer, ready to hold the child back if his or her choice will have harmful or detrimental results. This provides the child, the parent, and all others with an important sense of security and ease. The parent should not make the "police officer's role" the most prominent aspect of parenting. As much as possible, the parent wants the child to learn from his or her own experience what the real boundaries are. And the parent definitely does not want the child to think of the parent's contribution as primarily setting and enforcing laws.

4. The parent becomes teacher and guide. Some of the parent's most effective work will come after the choice has been put into action. Helping the child understand the consequences of the decision—whether positive or negative—is critical to learning.

5. The parent becomes cheerleader. Whenever the child makes a good attempt, and especially if the child makes a great decision, the parent goes all out to reinforce his or her effort.

Following this outline will help the child practice the decision-making strategies that will ensure long-term contentment.

■

THIS PROCESS REQUIRES A LOT OF TIME—AND PATIENCE

All parents know how much easier it is to make a decision for their child and enforce it: Read this book. Wear the red dress. Invite Billy instead of Johnny. True, such an approach is much easier and faster, but it does not equip the child to be a good decision maker in the future.

My wife, Marylyn, and I have three grown daughters, all married with children of their own. As a psychologist, I thought I knew a lot about parenting, but every time I'm around one of our daughters and their little ones, I am overwhelmed by the careful, patient way they go about teaching their kids to make wise choices.

Recently, I watched our oldest daughter, Lorrie, with her two-year-old twin boys. Both wanted to play with a toy truck at the same time. It would have been easy for Lorrie to resolve the problem for them. She could have turned on *Sesame Street* or tossed each boy a stuffed animal, and they would have quickly forgotten the truck. No temper tantrums, no hurt feelings, no fuss, no muss.

However, Lorrie chose the more time-consuming but instructive course. She got down on their level and said, "Boys, you both really want this truck, don't you? But you can't both have it at the same time, can you? So what if Warren takes this big bus for now and William keeps the truck for a few minutes? Then you can switch."

Unfortunately, that didn't work. But Lorrie hung in there: "Neither one of you wants to give up the truck, do you?" In their own form of two-year-old English, they let her know she had that one right. Then one of them said: "Both take truck." So for at least half a minute (an eternity for two-year-olds), they played with the truck together under Lorrie's watchful and delighted eye.

So what's the big deal? Did they really learn anything? You bet they did. First, they learned that some struggles are not easy to resolve. That's important! Without understanding that, they would grow up constantly looking for shortcuts and quick fixes. Second, they learned that compromise is not always easily obtained ("Bus for truck? Not on your life!"). Finally, they discovered an unusually advanced solution known as sharing. And though the sharing lasted no more than thirty seconds,

Lorrie's loving reinforcement of the boys undoubtedly made sharing a more likely choice in the future.

■

SOME PEOPLE ARE IN SYNC AT A YOUNG AGE

When you stay in sync with yourself, you will experience a tremendous amount of joy, even if all your decisions do not turn out as well as you would like. That's because deep satisfaction comes from making the choices that emerge from the center of your life experience. This is the highest form of human processing you will ever know. Without it, life becomes a drag. With it, life becomes spectacularly exciting.

One of the first clients I ever worked with was a seven-year-old girl named Karrin. She taught me as much about life as I taught her, maybe more. I didn't know it at the time, and Karrin didn't either, but she was incredibly in sync with herself. Her mother brought her to the counseling center of The University of Chicago, where I was an intern. She was assigned to me by random because I had an opening for a child client. As a matter of fact, that was the first week of my internship, and I had twenty-five openings for clients of any age. But I was fortunate indeed to have that bright little girl assigned to me.

I counseled her in the playroom, where there were a sandbox, puppets, and dozens of toys and games. My goal was to use *play* to form a relationship with Karrin. That may have been the easiest assignment of my professional life. Talk about "in sync"! That girl had an incredible ability to move inside herself and collect all the data for every choice, and though she sometimes took her time making choices, she inevitably made good ones.

And my relationship with her? I listened, reflected, asked a few questions—and marveled at how in tune Karrin was with herself. I often felt as in sync with her as I knew she was with herself. My only concern was whether she felt free to be seven years old, to play and enjoy herself, to grow up leisurely. I wonder if after all these years Karrin is a mother of her own seven-year-old. If she is, I suspect that the little girl is much like her mother was at the same age. After all, if you show me a great seven-year-old, I'll show you a great mother.

I have a grandson named Matt, also seven years old, who works the same kind of magic on a moment that Karrin did. He and I started something recently that we hope will survive for a long time. It was the day after he finished the first grade, and we spent the afternoon and evening playing every game we could come up with. We called them the Graduation Games, and we had a handsome trophy for the winner. We bowled, tried our luck at miniature golf, went to a batting cage, and played every kind of board game and card game. We kept score throughout the day, and when all the games were done, we had tied. Matt gets to keep the trophy for this year, but it says:

FIRST ANNUAL GRADUATION GAMES
TIE—MATT AND GRANDPA

I loved that day, and I think he did too. I wonder if he enjoyed getting to know me on such a deep level as I enjoyed getting to know him. I watched him at lunch when he was ordering his food, and I watched him deciding what he wanted to do next. And there it was again! That same ability to access his internal data, to make good choices that even grown-ups are fortunate to make. When a seven-year-old shows this capacity, you know that a mom and dad have done a fabulous job of raising this young person.

■

YOU CAN LEARN ALL THIS EVEN AS AN ADULT

I have seen hundreds of people in psychotherapy who were totally ineffective decision makers. They had little contact with the deep, intimate, internal parts of themselves. They never thought to include in their data accumulation all their thoughts and feelings. Or they gave too much power to an outside source, perhaps a parent or a boss.

What I do is teach them how to gather data. In a sense, I have to repeat the parenting process. I have to become for them what our daughter Lorrie was to her twins.

I remember Jeanie, whose only consideration for any choice was "whatever Mom would do in this situation." Both parents encouraged her to copy her mother's approach to life almost totally. No one ever asked Jeanie what she thought, what she wanted, or what her goals were. She didn't ask herself those questions either. It wasn't surprising, then, that she dressed like her mother, fixed her hair like her, handled conflict like her, and often treated her husband like her mother treated her father.

Jeanie had incredible gifts and attributes, but she wasn't coming close to realizing her potential. Even more important, she was seriously depressed and light-years away from contentment. She needed to open up communication lines with her feelings and thoughts in relation to every choice. But more than anything else, she needed to wrest the decision-making rights and responsibilities from her mother. She desperately needed to get back inside her control booth. If she didn't, she was destined to live a terribly compromised life.

"I've just never been taught how to listen to myself," she said.

"It's seems to me that you've closed the lid on your inner world for so long that it's stuck shut," I told her. "But that doesn't mean you can't learn to open it and hear everything that's going on inside yourself."

I spent hour after hour asking questions, clarifying, and focusing Jeanie's inner happenings as best I knew how. Sometimes she was afraid to say what she thought and felt, especially if it deviated from what her mother had taught her to think and feel. I tried to give her the freedom to entertain her true thoughts and feelings and to let them mix with data from other sources. Eventually, she began letting some of this information in. Then she learned to turn up the volume a little. Finally, she started paying real attention to it.

Jeanie's breakthrough issue involved the degree to which she would allow herself to be successful at work. For four or five years, she had worked for a sales organization. She had experienced a reasonable level of achievement, but when her sales leveled off for eighteen months, she had to look carefully at how she was holding herself back.

"What did your mother tell you about success and achievement, especially as they relate to work?" I asked her.

"Now that you mention it, she told me—not in so many words, of course—that I shouldn't be more successful than she was. For years she worked as a paralegal, and she made a decent salary, but certainly not what you'd call lucrative. I always got the sense that I shouldn't aim too high, that I shouldn't overshadow her. She wanted to be the successful one."

"It sounds like your mother's ideas about being too successful are dictating your level of motivation," I said. "And you're limiting your success level at a point where your mother will not feel outdone."

When Jeanie began to understand that her mother was in charge of her control booth—even in the area of business—she determined that she would make a change. Of course, her mother's presence was mostly a matter of Jeanie's thinking. But when the eviction proceedings were complete, her sales volume began to climb at an incredible rate. In one year, she doubled her previous twelve-month high. And although she periodically felt tempted to retreat, especially when her mother expressed disapproval, Jeanie never yielded her decision-making powers.

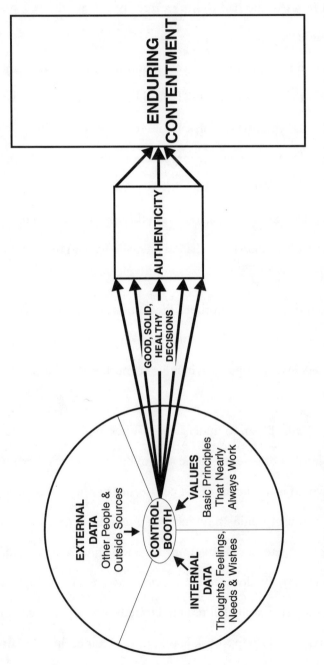

The Only Path to Enduring Contentment

■

IT'S NEVER TOO LATE

If you see yourself—even a little bit—in Jeanie's story, you are probably out of sync with your deepest self, and you may have never developed appreciation for the person you were created to become. If someone else occupies your control booth, all the unique perspectives of your inner being may have been lost. There is no way you can be satisfied with your life, no way that you can experience real joy.

But I am delighted to tell you that I have watched hundreds of people reconnect with their true selves, and this always begins with the ability to make sound decisions moment by moment. Authenticity involves one conscious, competent choice after another. Every decision is essentially different, but the process is virtually always the same:

1. Determine the decision you need to make.
2. Identify which data sources bear on this decision.
3. Listen to these data sources logging in with their input.
4. Evaluate all the data and, using your values and principles, make your choice.
5. Follow through with your choice, and carefully study the consequences in light of intended goals and desires.

Deep-down contentment and satisfaction come from a sense of being in sync with yourself. When you have never learned how to make clear, dependable decisions, when you are a passive responder to someone else's choices, you may enjoy brief moments of happiness that come from letting others run your life, but they will soon fade. However, when you learn to make healthy choices all along the way, when you become authentically yourself, you set yourself up for lasting contentment.

■

chapter five

RECOGNIZE THE CRITICAL IMPORTANCE OF YOUR CONTROL BOOTH

☐ Your boss plops a pile of work on your desk at four o'clock on Friday afternoon. "I need it finished by Monday morning," he says. You know it's not fair. None of your colleagues will be forced to work the entire weekend. But as you load up your briefcase, you don't say a word.

Your friend sets you up on a blind date even though you deplore blind dates. You really don't want to go, but you go anyway.

You're in college, and it's time to declare a major. You're sure theater is for you, but Mom and Dad, who are paying the tuition, insist there is no future in that and are convinced you would make a great accountant. So you enroll in Accounting 101.

Your wedding is fast approaching, and you are starting to have grave doubts. It's not a matter of jitters or cold feet. You have some legitimate concerns about your spouse-to-be. But everyone says you make such a wonderful couple—and besides, the invitations are already out—so you swallow your fears and proceed as if nothing is wrong.

Why is it that when we're confronted with something we don't want to do, we often remain silent? Why do we move ahead with a decision, even though our inner world screams to do the opposite? What causes us to concede to others' wishes at the expense of our own?

It's all a matter of who is in our control booth.

In the last chapter, we discussed the importance of making wise, authentic decisions moment by moment. And we said that a key to that process is standing in the middle of your control booth—the command center of your brain, where the data are sorted, assessed, and evaluated. When you allow someone else to seize control of this critical operation, you will not make decisions that are true to yourself, and then you're sure to thwart any chance of contentment.

So are you inside or outside your control booth? Are you making your own choices and decisions? If you're not—and most individuals aren't—why aren't you? If you discover who occupies your control booth and what keeps you locked out, you will have a decidedly better chance of reclaiming it as your own, becoming the person you were born to be, and ultimately finding meaningful contentment.

■

THE MAIN REASON WE'RE SHUT OUT OF OUR CONTROL BOOTH

When we are confused and uncertain about how our self-worth is determined, our most frequent response is to hand over our controls to someone we think determines our value and worth as an individual. This person is often a parent, but it can be almost anyone—a sibling, teacher, coworker, close friend, even a child.

Our need to feel good about ourselves is so all-consuming that whatever or whomever has the authority to decide our worth has the power to dictate the rules of our lives. Consequently, that institution or person can commandeer our control booth and ultimately determine how we make decisions.

For most of my life, I gave my dad enormous power over me. He was a commanding figure—intelligent, persuasive, idealistic, and deeply confident. He had incredibly high expectations for me from the time I was born until he died. I desperately wanted to please him and meet his lofty goals for me. As a man whose education had been cut short after only eight years, he wanted me to live the life he had been deprived of, to rise to the academic heights he had never been able to reach, and to do all of this nearby so he could fully enjoy my progress.

I sought Dad's affirmation and approval. He let me know that I was extremely important to him, but he failed to convey that he loved me for who I was and not for what I achieved or how I performed. Don't get me wrong, I never doubted that I mattered to him, but I always sensed that his love was conditional, that he would value me highly as long as I lived up to his dreams for me.

As a result, I spent much of my life allowing him to be in charge of my control booth. Now and then, he would let me in there with him to make minor decisions relating to school—as long as all the big issues were under his full control. I let him in there because I started thinking early on that he was the one who determined my worth. I wanted him to think well of me, or perhaps more important, I didn't want him to disapprove of me. I became convinced I could feel good about myself only when he thought I was worth something.

Let's be clear about this: There is nothing wrong with wanting to please others. Humans seem to be wired with the desire for affirmation and approval from other people, especially those most important to us. *The problem comes when we look to someone else to decide whether we're valuable and worthy.* Then we have offered that person the command post of our lives. In my case, I was convinced that my dad was the one who could say whether I was good or not. Since I wanted so much to feel good about myself, and since he could decide if I had the right to feel that way, I played by his rules. I made the decisions he wanted me to make.

■

WHO IS VYING FOR CONTROL OF YOUR LIFE?

You don't have to look hard to find persons and groups that want to monopolize your decision making and live your life for you. It is rare to find someone *uninterested* in dictating what you should think and feel. Individuals or groups needing you to behave according to their plan will try to influence you to do things their way.

People do this to make themselves feel more secure. If you think and act the way they think you should, they feel less anxious about the way they are. Moreover, if they are able to get you to behave toward them in a certain way, they start believing that you will be an enduring source of positive feelings about them. You become a vital pawn in their achievement of emotional strength.

Consider a few people and groups that frequently vie for control over our decision making:

PARENTS

I mentioned my power struggle with my dad, and I suppose millions of people find themselves in a similar tug-of-war for control with either their mother or father or both. If your mother repeatedly tells you what you feel instead of helping you focus inside to discover for yourself what you feel, she may be at the center of your control room. If your father always tells you what to do, refusing to give you freedom to choose anything for yourself, he may be in control of your life.

The power you give to others is as strong as your belief about their role as the determiner of your value and worth. That's why parents often inhabit your control booth—they are usually the significant people in your life, and you look to them for validation. If you have questions about your worth, and if you're convinced your value depends on your parents' appraisal of you, they will have enormous power over you.

PEER GROUPS

When your friends try to tell you how to behave and think, they may be attempting to muscle you out of your control room. If your peers punish you when you don't let them control you—excluding you, putting you down, trying to make you feel guilty or inferior—they are indeed trying to take control of your life.

EMPLOYERS

Unless you are in a top executive position or have a job that requires a high level of creativity, your employer probably doesn't want you to think much for yourself. It's not that she doesn't want you to use your brain; she would just prefer that you follow procedures, obey rules, and comply with established guidelines. It's simply easier for your employer if you automatically do as she says.

POLITICAL PARTIES

Many parties run ads on television that make one thing clear: They want you to vote the way they want you to vote. They don't really want you to study and critique the issues. Essentially, they want you to rubber-stamp their decisions.

SOME CHURCHES AND SYNAGOGUES

Many religious groups and places of worship are tremendously helpful and affirming; others demand conformity and compliance in order for you to be accepted. The message they transmit is, "Think like we think, and then we will treat you as a person of great value." Of course, if you hold a position that varies from theirs, your value will diminish in their eyes. And to the degree that you think their opinion of you determines your true value, you may consider letting them have control of your decisions.

This list could go on and on. Virtually every person and group you encounter wants you to think as they do, feel as they do, choose as they do. If you have to be totally inauthentic to be the way they want you to be, that's okay with them. But doing this is equivalent to giving them the real power in your life. And it will *never* result in lasting contentment.

■

YOU MAY RESORT TO BARTERING

If you're dealing with people who have something you vitally need, they will often try to trade it for some measure of control over you. This is called bartering, which on an emotional level usually involves trading acceptance and affirmation in exchange for decision-making rights.

For example, the mother we discussed in an earlier chapter responded with a soothing tone of voice and a smiling face when her baby stopped crying. This is a form of primitive bartering. As we get older, the bartering deals become more complex. We may act quiet and reserved when we sense that someone we admire wants us to be that way. Or we may not voice a differing opinion to someone we want to please.

When someone has something you need, be careful how you barter! Consider trying to get along without what he or she is trying to trade you because giving up control of your center is extremely dangerous to your emotional health.

One client said to me recently, "I have some kind of implicit deal going with virtually every important person in my life. I put in long hours at work and don't buck the system so I'll keep getting kudos from my boss. I'm getting my master's degree because my dad tells me I'll go farther with more education. I take my girlfriend to fancy restaurants and buy her expensive gifts because I sense she likes me better when I spend money on her. In order to get all these people to think well of me, I've given away a lot of my decision-making freedom."

I could relate to what he was saying. At one point in my life, I wanted to be liked more than I wanted to be authentic. I had become convinced that being liked automatically meant being popular, and popularity automatically meant I could feel good about myself. So I set out to be liked by everyone. Unfortunately, I lived my life trying to satisfy my fraternity brothers, fellow student council members, every girl I found attractive, the professors who would determine my academic future—virtually every person I knew.

When I was a graduate student, I figured out that I had given away almost all of my control. Then it was simply a matter of trying to be the person I had implicitly promised to be. With one group of persons, I was open and revealing because that's what I perceived they wanted from me. With another group, I was more serious and studious. I became proficient at reading people, groups, and situations to see what our "deal" was. So eager was I for the payoff from them that I tried desperately to keep my end of the bargains. For being what they wanted, my classmates and friends elected me student body president, honored me in several ways, and put me at the center of my social group. But the payoffs almost always turned out to be superficial, short-term, and disappointing.

I'm sure you understand what I'm saying because most of us have at least one or two people with whom we're bartering. In exchange for their attributions of value—or some other reward—we will think, feel, do, and be the way they want us to.

■

SOMETIMES THE STAKES ARE EXTREMELY HIGH

I have had thousands of people in therapy who had surrendered possession of their control booth to someone else—sometimes to several people or groups. The result was almost always a deep feeling of emptiness or hopelessness, resulting in depression. You can't relinquish control of your life—or barter it away—without perilous consequences.

A twenty-year-old woman named Michele came to me for therapy because she had "sold out" to her authoritative father. He was not only imposing and forceful, but also incredibly wealthy. He owned several companies, and Michele worked in the marketing department for one of them. Her father had strong opinions on virtually everything, and he made it clear that if she wanted his respect and encouragement, she should adopt his opinions, values, beliefs, preferences, and wishes.

He had a lot to offer, and that's why she yielded total control of her life to him. If she hadn't, she would have risked losing his approval and affirmation, her job, and possibly her future inheritance (that was one of his bartering ploys). She also risked upsetting the family equilibrium and forfeiting all the status and rewards that came with being the daughter of a rich man. So she became nearly a carbon copy of him. But before long, she felt awkward in the role—too rigid, bullheaded, angry, and defensive. She became less and less attractive to herself and to others, especially men in her age group. She was like a robot with a control room under her father's total domination.

So we set out to rectify all this. Was it easy? Not on your life. She knew him well enough to be convinced that if she tried to become an authentic person, all deals with him would be off. He wasn't bluffing; he would take back all his bargaining chips.

We talked at length about the control-booth concept. She agreed that he was in charge, but every time we talked about reclaiming her decision-making powers, her anxiety became almost unmanageable.

"What's the worst that could happen if you were to start living according to your own beliefs, feelings, and values?" I asked. "Would the trade-off—authenticity and deep-down contentment—be worth what you might give up?"

"Daddy would make my life miserable. He would make me feel bad for going my own way. He'd make me feel like a rotten daughter. He'd stop making payments on my BMW, that's for sure. And he might tell my supervisor to demote me—or fire me. I just couldn't do it."

"Then are you resigned to having someone else control you as long as you live—or at least as long as your father lives?"

"I don't want that, but there's just too much at stake. Besides, it would hurt my mother too. She's so into peacemaking and family harmony. She *always* takes Daddy's side."

I suspected Michele's wasn't the only control booth her father occupied.

I tried a different approach to shake Michele out of her compliant, subservient role. "It seems as if your father's approval and gifts are given with as many conditions as his business deals. It's as if he says, 'Do and be what I want you to do and be, and I will give you worth and favor and an exciting career path.'"

She remained unswayed. For her, the threatened loss of everything her father offered made her feel as anxious as if she were about to lose her life.

I worked as hard as I knew how with Michele, but I have no wonderful outcome to report. The sorry fact is that she quit coming to me when her anxiety skyrocketed. Her courage to squarely face the struggle had been insufficient, at least to that point. She made her choice—she bartered away control of her life.

Powerful people and powerful groups often threaten to take away all kinds of rewards if you show signs of evicting them from your control room. One father of a thirty-year-old man I was counseling called me to say, "If my son doesn't reconsider his independent ways, I am done with him."

The fundamental goal of your life must be to live every moment at the center of your control booth. If you forfeit this right, you will never experience joy and contentment. How could you? Your center would be essentially vacant.

■

IF YOU WANT TO RETAKE YOUR CONTROL BOOTH, EXPECT RESISTANCE

I've spent decades working with people on this issue, and I know that "the intruders" who are being thrown out of the control booth do not often go quietly. When you think of taking control back from specific people, expect fierce counterattacks. The deal you made with these people—a long time ago perhaps—was probably never put into words, but the terms are clear to both sides. If you threaten to change the arrangement, the other person is likely to make a huge fuss, even insinuating all kinds of possible retribution.

Sometimes these powerful persons use guilt and shame in an attempt to get their way. One of my clients used to let her mother have full command of her control room, but then she decided to reclaim it. The mother felt betrayed that her daughter would go back on their deal, and she was intent on punishing her daughter. She told her daughter, "You used to be such a wonderful daughter, so loving and easy to get along with, but now it's like you just don't care about me at all. I miss the old you. Do you even love me anymore?" The fact that the compliant daughter was for years chronically depressed, felt lost and empty, and was just beginning to feel good again didn't seem to matter.

Threats of retribution happen frequently in marriage when one partner decides to regain control. Many years ago, I saw a man and a woman who had created a miserable marriage out of a series of bartering agreements. The husband, a powerful and wealthy businessman, had worked a deal with his wife in which she was to be a servant, nursemaid, and nonperson. In exchange, he would allow her to have "his" kids, use some of "his" money, share in some of "his" status, and even use "his" last name.

Obviously, the arrangement could never work for long. She was a nonentity. She didn't even know where her control booth was, let alone how to regain it. Eventually, their marriage began to sour. She lost all interest in being sexually intimate with him, and as far as the husband could see, that was a gross violation of their deal. He wasn't going to stand for it any longer, so they came to therapy.

Much to his chagrin, she took tiny steps toward becoming her own person. For the first time since they had been married, someone was asking her what she thought, what she felt, and what she wanted. As she mustered her courage to retake control of her life, the husband became more and more threatened by the broken deal. Mind you, their deal was thoroughly unhealthy and their marriage was based on all kinds of bartering, but from his point of view, a deal was a deal.

He immediately threatened divorce. He had never mentioned divorce before, so the new threat frightened his wife. She had a lot to lose—the family solidarity, the status, the money, the sense of being a loyal deal-keeper, perhaps even the children.

But she also began to recognize that the only way she and their marriage could ever experience real happiness was for her to stand again at the helm of her inner life. She struggled for months before she determined the direction she would take. It was a struggle between a financially secure emotional death and a materially insecure authentic life.

When she eventually chose to regain her personhood, her husband stopped his threats. He had been blindly committed to the old deal, but it wasn't long before he recognized the exciting possibilities of a new arrangement—an arrangement between two healthy human beings. The new deal required an enormous amount of growth and adjustment for both of them, but with guidance and encouragement along the way, they stayed at the task.

Of course, not all situations have such a happy ending. Evicting someone from your control booth usually incites turmoil and upheaval. Don't give in to threats or resistance. If you stand firm and recapture your control booth, you'll be well on your way toward authenticity and contentment.

■

OVERCOMING THE USE OF DEFENSES

When you allow other persons or groups to take over your control booth, it is often difficult to break the habit, to change the pattern, to begin choosing and deciding for yourself. Usually, that's because you have kept yourself almost totally unaware. You may have maintained your innocence, failing to acknowledge the discrepancies between the person you were pretending to be and the person you truly are deep down.

As a human being you are largely unable to confront consciously any evidence that you are inauthentic. It is a fact about you that you tend to blur through distortion or sometimes even total denial. You simply cannot admit that you are inauthentic. The blurring and denying are often referred to as defense mechanisms. They keep you unaware of your duplicitous nature—the fact that you have made a deal to trade your true self for the acceptance and validation you think someone else can grant you.

These defenses become more and more ingrained as you continue to use them. And finally, when you decide that you want desperately to become authentic again, to retake your control booth, you have to move through emotional territory that you have for years masked and even obliterated with these defenses.

Consider the young woman who was sexually abused between the ages of ten and fifteen by her stepfather. If she had been totally in charge of her control booth, she would have made an enormous scene and stopped the abuse the moment it began. However, she was an emotionally vulnerable person as a ten-year-old, and her stepfather was a significant figure in her life. She falsely but understandably believed that he had the power to determine her worth. So he dominated her into making a deal with him. In response to his false promise of helping her feel valuable, she let him take control of an incredibly intimate part of her life.

But by the time she reached age fifteen, the horrible pain of her deal may have demanded that she totally change this arrangement. And let's assume she vowed to retake her position at the center of her control system. Do not underestimate how crucial this would be for her emotional health—or how difficult.

The point here is that to move back into her control booth, she has to traverse emotional territory that for five years she had managed with denial and distortion. When feelings have been repeatedly manipulated in this way, it is often difficult for someone to register them consciously in their true form. She has to focus intently on her feelings, try desperately to stop managing them in manipulative ways, and see them for exactly what they are.

I have watched many courageous people fight with all their might to reclaim their control booth. No other human experience requires more courage and deserves more support. It is a struggle for the very meaning of life.

■

THE THRILL OF VICTORY

One of the biggest surprises of my life was recapturing my control booth from my dad, whom I told you about earlier in this chapter. I grew up in a Protestant denomination. My dad was extremely involved with this church group, and much of his life revolved around his church responsibilities. From the time I was ten years old, I had reservations about the denomination, but our whole family attended this church for years out of deference to my dad.

Marylyn and I had been married for several years and all three of our girls had been born when we felt the strong conviction that we needed to leave the denomination. I was in an awkward position. That church meant the world to my dad! I summoned my courage to tell him that we would be looking for another church.

I will never forget the Sunday afternoon I sat down with him in the living room of my parents' home. I remember that conversation as if it was yesterday. It was a turning point in my journey toward authenticity.

"Dad," I said nervously, "I need to talk to you about this church matter."

"Oh?" he said. "What is it, Son?"

I swallowed hard and pressed on. "I just wish you could trust Marylyn and me to make a good decision about the best place for us and the girls to be, even if that means going to a different church."

There was a long pause, and I could virtually see the wheels spinning in his large head.

"Trust you?" he said finally. "I trust you more than any other person on earth."

I was taken aback. "But, Dad, can you handle me—and my family—leaving the church?"

"I'd hate for you to leave the church," he said, "but if that's what you need to do, I want you to do it."

I couldn't believe my ears! I had done it. I had discussed with my dad one of the most tense issues between us. I had taken a step back into my control booth, and he had not raised a finger to stop me. To his credit, my dad never showed a single ounce of inconsistency through the years about his statement; he never tried to make me feel guilty or convince me that I had made the wrong decision.

That surprise changed my life enormously—not just because Marylyn and I felt free to leave a difficult church situation, but because I experienced how refreshing and renewing it is to retake a part of myself that I thought I had dealt away. The fact was that it was mine for the asking. Sometimes, we only *think* our control booth is occupied by someone else. When we assert our rights, we discover that we have essentially held ourselves hostage. We have been according tremendous power to what I call *shadow intruders*.

But as one who had to fight to regain control of my decision-making ability, I can tell you it is absolutely impossible to experience anything more than pseudohappiness if you allow anyone but yourself to navigate your life. Surrendering your control booth to someone else often takes place quietly and in ways difficult to comprehend. And the struggle to regain control can be intense.

But I promise you this: If you determine to find your way back to the center of yourself, you will get there. And when you do, it may be the single most important accomplishment of your life. For you will discover yourself. You will be in sync. You will come to know soul-satisfying contentment.

chapter six

■

BREAK FREE
FROM OLD ENTANGLEMENTS

When you discover that your life is being lived primarily in response to what others want from you, contentment is sure to be in short supply. The only way you can remedy this situation is to move back to the center of yourself. You must begin again—you must literally start over in trying to be as authentically you as you know how.

This effort to build a new life is often referred to as *rebirth*. The idea of being born again is precisely what the process is all about. But sometimes the term *born again* is confusing to people. They think of it as something overly spiritual, maybe even magical, and they want to run from it.

My psychological training and experience have convinced me that rebirth is crucial to an understanding of authenticity. If you have given up possession of your control booth and are no longer making one fully informed decision after another from the center of you, you will not experience contentment until you regain control of your life. This often requires a complex and excruciatingly painful process that is accurately referred to as being born again.

■

THE FIRST STEP TOWARD REBIRTH IS TO EXPERIENCE YOUR LOSTNESS

To move toward authenticity and contentment, we must first be aware that we are lost. We must acknowledge that our strategies to find a meaningful, satisfying life have not succeeded. We must recognize that we have handed over control to other people or institutions. Tragically, most people do not recognize their lostness until some crisis occurs—a threatened divorce, the loss of a job, a bankruptcy, a child who gets in trouble with the law, a serious health problem.

Or perhaps a person will have an emotional crisis in which the longing for deep-down contentment becomes intolerable. For many people, this happens at middle age. For years, they chase all the things they were told would bring contentment—education, awards, success in their career, the accumulation of possessions. But they slowly come to realize that all those things have not brought lasting satisfaction.

Although distressing, crises like these can serve a valuable purpose. Such painful events demand that you become acutely aware of your inner state. If you are lost, pain often helps you recognize your condition so you will take action to improve it.

This is the same principle that applies to alcoholics. Often a person with a drinking addiction will not seek help—and often will not even recognize the problem—until catastrophe occurs. Only after a drunk driving arrest, bankruptcy, divorce, or some other crisis will the alcoholic acknowledge the problem and consider a new course.

Occasionally, individuals are able to recognize their emotional lostness without having to suffer excruciating pain. This recognition is usually the result of someone else challenging them to reflect upon and analyze their life. The challenge might come from an older, wiser person who warns them about pursuing the wrong things.

A person who is most successfully living the lost life is in the worst danger of all. This is a critical point. If a person never endures a crisis, he or she may plod through life believing all is well and never evaluate his or her life and take action to secure contentment. This is why it is counterproductive to constantly bail out someone whose pain might force a change. As coldhearted as it may sound, the person who perpetually runs up debts, mismanages money, and then wants to borrow money from you may actually be helped by going bankrupt. That may be the wake-up call needed to make fundamental changes that will correct long-term deficiencies and ensure the pattern is not repeated in the future.

■

THE MOST IMPORTANT REQUIREMENT FOR REBIRTH IS TO EXPERIENCE UNCONDITIONAL POSITIVE REGARD

Review in your mind what keeps you out of your control booth. What causes you to give up the right to choose in every moment who you will be and what you will do? This surrender takes place in your bartering deals with people and groups who want to have some power over you. Since they have something you want—usually some form of positive regard for you—and since they will give it only if you meet their conditions, you make a deal with them. This whole process starts because of your need to feel valuable, worthwhile, and affirmed.

Whatever deals you've made were disastrous for two reasons. First, you bartered away your most valuable treasure—your own personhood, your ability to be fully who you are. Second, you bartered this precious gift for something cheap—*conditional* love. This kind of exchange is enticing because it appears to offer something you want: approval, validation, and acceptance. But conditional love comes with strings attached and ultimately will fail to provide emotional security.

When your sense of worth is based on conditional factors, you set yourself up to be inauthentic. When others place stipulations on your feelings of value, any contentment you achieve will be ephemeral. You experience only pseudohappiness, suffer anxiety about the future, and wonder who exactly you really are in the world. You are desperately in need of rebirth.

Hundreds of people have come to me in this predicament—businessmen whose sense of worth hinged on getting a promotion, meeting next month's quota, or receiving a commendation from the boss; wives whose sense of significance derived from any gratitude or praise that might come from their husband and kids; pastors and church leaders whose self-esteem was contingent upon a successful program or the approval of their parishioners.

What these people needed is the same thing that every person on earth needs if they want to undergo the kind of shift that leads to contentment. They needed to experience *unconditional positive regard*—the assurance that their worth as persons is permanent and will never be taken away. When fully understood and received, this incredible quality makes personal and emotional rebirth possible.

■

THE POWER OF UNCONDITIONAL POSITIVE REGARD

When you encounter unconditional love, all emotional deals designed to produce self-worth become unnecessary. This kind of positive regard is given without expectation of anything in return. It is totally devoid of exchanges and trades, what I refer to as mutuality and reciprocity.

Most emotional deals between humans are based on all kinds of conditions. But some people do freely offer this unconditional positive regard. Think about an emotionally healthy mother who is so secure within herself that she doesn't have to control her kids, her husband, or anyone else. She is squarely planted in her own control booth, deeply in touch with her inner workings, and capable of helping her children or her spouse come to this same healthy place.

Perhaps no earthly moment is more emotionally healthy than when a mother is nursing her child, holding him or her tenderly, looking down into her baby's face, and offering pure and unrestrained love. Any mother who can love a child without smothering him and nurture a child without needing to control him is a healthy mother with an inexhaustible supply of unconditional positive regard.

Mothers and fathers who have experienced unconditional love for themselves can pass it along to their children. This is perhaps the most precious gift they can give their sons and daughters, for it almost guarantees a deep, unshakable sense of worth. While parents are in the best position to impart this quality to their children, sometimes emotionally healthy relatives or friends can do the same.

I saw a seventeen-year-old boy named Mitch for therapy. He had come from an extremely troubled home, and he had many difficult issues to work through. He was stumbling badly in his efforts to grow up. But despite the challenges he faced, I was almost positive he would overcome his struggles and go on to live a great life. Why did I have such confidence in him? Because he had experienced unconditional love, and he accepted it for himself.

"I detect a rare quality in you," I told Mitch one day.

He sat up a little straighter and said, "Really? What do you mean?"

"It seems that you have the ability to accept yourself and to know that your value as a person is not at stake, regardless of any mistakes you might make or how other people might view you."

Mitch looked a little sheepish. He was unaccustomed to people pointing out his positive attributes. "Well, yeah," he said with a grin. "I hadn't really thought about it like that, but I guess you're right."

"As I said, that's a rare quality," I went on. "So how do you think you developed it?"

"My uncle Doug," he said without hesitation. "I don't know where I'd be without him. You know how messed up my family is. Well, my uncle saw that I was getting into trouble, and he decided to take me under his wing. We go fishing or shoot hoops or just hang out. I just always know he accepts me as I am."

"So how does he communicate that he accepts you?"

"It's like no matter what I'm going through or wherever I am emotionally, he treats me the same. Oh, he still comes down on me when I blow it. He tells me flat out when he thinks I'm messin' up. But that doesn't change his opinion of me, you know? He cares about me no matter what."

As he told me more, I recognized that this uncle had consistently treated Mitch with great dignity, communicated his affection, demonstrated unconditional caring, and played a quiet but powerful role in his nephew's emotional and spiritual development.

If you find a friend, pastor, therapist, teacher, coach, or anyone else who demonstrates this kind of unconditional love, you've found a treasure. Spend as much time with this person as possible. Receiving unqualified positive regard is the best way to develop inner security and a solid self-worth.

■

THE LINK BETWEEN FAITH AND UNCONDITIONAL POSITIVE REGARD

What if you could establish once and for all that your worth is beyond measure? What if there was no way your worth could ever be diminished? What if you knew that there is absolutely no need for you to ever make another soul-sacrificing emotional deal with a parent, boss, spouse, or peer group? Would this change everything about your life strategy?

When I discovered as an adult that unconditional love is the fundamental tenet of the Christian faith—the faith I was raised in—I was shocked and incredulous. Nobody had bothered to clarify this unbelievably good news during my growing-up years. Despite all the sermons I listened to and the classes I attended, I had never understood this concept. I'd heard phrases such as *God's grace, unmerited favor,* and *sacrificial love,* but I never *experienced* these ideas. During my childhood, no one ever modeled for me the kind of love or regard that is free of stipulations.

As an adult, well after I had become a psychologist, I came to understand that when we place our faith in God, our value and worth is established for all time. His love for us is total—and totally unconditional. There is nothing we can do to make Him love us any more or any less. This good news is the clearest example of unconditional positive regard, the very dynamic that makes it possible to return to your control booth and be "born again." And this incredible truth of unconditional love is presented as a fact on the basis of a historical event—the birth, death, and resurrection of Jesus Christ two thousand years ago. It is not as though you can buy this gift or somehow control it. You can only believe it or not believe it. You can read about it in its purest, most powerful form in the New Testament.

Unconditional positive regard is the most potent psychological force in creating the conditions for people to freely move back into the center of their lives, and it is fully available in a consistent and enduring way in a faith system that is readily available to anyone.

■

A BIBLICAL CASE IN POINT

One of the Bible's most delightful and dynamic passages is a parable Jesus told about unconditional love. It stands as a pivotal teaching in human history, and it focuses on the source of the unconditional love that is so vital to the attainment of authenticity. I suppose most people in the western world have heard the story, but I for one can never get enough of it. It is central to my life and work.

An abbreviated version of the story goes like this: A man had two sons. The younger son asked for his share of the father's estate and, receiving it, went to a far country and squandered everything he had been given on riotous, irresponsible living. He finally bottomed out. He decided to return home to see if he could become a hired hand on his father's farm.

As he walked down the road toward home, his dad saw him at a great distance and ran to meet him. The father embraced and kissed his son. The son's rehearsed speech was interrupted by the dad, who was filled with deep caring and overwhelming joy. The father welcomed him home with great celebration.

The older son returned home from working in the fields, and he was told that a party was being thrown for his younger brother, who had returned. This older son was deeply offended, feeling that he had always worked conscientiously to please his father—yet there had never been a celebration of his life. He refused to join the party.

The father went out to talk with him and listened carefully to the deep frustration of his older son. "And he said to him, 'Son you are always with me, and all that I have is yours. It was right that we should make merry and be glad, for your brother was dead and is alive again, and was lost and is found.'" (Luke 15:31–32).

The father in this story, of course, represents God. Jesus is saying that God is like this—always more loving and compassionate than we expect. He is the one who comes down the road to meet us when we have run into a pit of emptiness. And He is the one who lets us know that our worth is never dependent upon our achievements, nor is it diminished by our mistakes. It is this powerful expression of our permanent worth that sets us free to move back into our control booth.

You can imagine the joy a story like this brings to a psychologist like me. At the very moment we so desperately need a powerful infusion of unconditional love, right in the center of our pain and lostness, God comes down the road to meet us. This is the mind-boggling love and acceptance that makes authenticity possible.

■

YOU NEED A GUIDE TO LEAD YOU

People who have spent years entangled in relationships in which emotional deals were involved find the long trip back to their centers extremely difficult. They need leadership from someone who has already achieved authenticity and is willing to show the way.

To whom should you look when you need a guide? My question is not whether you should seek out a friend, a psychotherapist, a mentor, or a spiritual leader. My question has to do with the emotional health of any prospective guide whose help you might request. What matters most is whether the potential guide has personally experienced unconditional positive regard and can freely offer it to you. Is the person securely in charge of his or her own control booth? Is the individual authentic and genuine? I talk at length in Chapter 9 about how you can know if a person is in sync, and that information may help you identify someone who can help you in your quest for contentment.

■

YOU ALSO NEED A CHEERING SECTION

Marylyn and I have great respect for Young Life, an organization that helps high school kids develop strong values and a commitment to spiritual faith. So when friends invited us to visit a Young Life camp, we didn't think twice. Marylyn and I both went to the camp, which sat on the edge of the water in British Columbia and could be reached only by air or sea.

When we arrived by boat one sunny July afternoon, I experienced one of the most inspirational events of my life. A quarter-mile path led from the boat landing to the camp, and the campers from the previous week were lined up along this path. As we walked past them, they clapped and cheered for us, and the applause and hoopla echoed into the distance. They were cheering for *all* of us—every new person coming to the camp.

As I moved along the path that day, I could not help thinking how much we all need a cheering section. We need to know that people are on our side, pulling for us, standing with us. Whether this section be filled by a mixture of old and new friends, close family members, teammates from our softball league, or fellow staff members from work, we get such a lift from knowing that others are eager for us to do well. And I can tell you that no one is more deserving of support and encouragement than a person who is trying to achieve authenticity.

I have watched thousands of people try to retake their control room. Many have succeeded, but far too many have not. In fact, I can think of dozens of persons who were never able to free themselves from all the emotional baggage in their lives. They simply gave up and settled for their out-of-syncness. Sometimes the only difference between success and failure is a powerful cheering section.

A woman named Julie came to me several years ago complaining of a "stuck" marriage, a sense of helplessness, and a chronically depressed mood. I talked to her for three or four sessions and gave her some psychological tests. Finally, we began to pinpoint her problem.

Julie had traded her inner freedom for a life situation that others might envy. Her husband, Ben, was quite wealthy when they married, and they had everything money could buy. Julie had two little girls and an older boy, and all three were physically healthy and doing well in school. Her responsibility was to raise the children and participate in the big life Ben was living. Yet he was totally obsessed with his work and almost completely unavailable to her. He was heavily involved with politics and social functions, and their life was overwhelmingly stressful seven days a week.

Julie didn't feel like an equal partner in their fast-lane life. In fact, she felt that it was not the life she would choose at all. She had no interest in politics, and she found the social events boring and snobbish. She wanted a much simpler existence—and she longed for more intimacy with her husband.

Julie had been a passive partner in the development of this unsatisfying life. She felt such a strong need for her husband's acceptance that she kept her mouth shut and went along with what he wanted. She eventually decided that she wanted to make some changes in her life, but she very much wanted to stay married too. Her challenge was immense. Her husband was so powerful—and she perceived herself as insignificant. She badly needed the inspiration of a cheering section.

I encouraged Julie to consider group therapy. I suspected that the group I had in mind for her would serve as the support network she lacked. She agreed. Over the following few months, she became more and more open with the nine other men and women in the group. They asked her all kinds of questions, challenged her to think deeply about herself, and shepherded her back to her control room. And they never missed a chance to cheer for her and tell her how proud they were of her heroic courage.

This process was incredibly frightening—and therapeutic—for Julie. She became clear about her needs and her position on innumerable issues. She received unconditional regard from her group members. And she gained the fortitude to speak her mind with her husband and let him know precisely where she stood on any issue. Perhaps most important, she told Ben she would no longer go along with the life he wanted, which she found so unsatisfying, and she asked him to be more involved with her.

There were times when Ben threatened, times when he refused, times when he wouldn't speak to Julie for days. But her cheering section never waned in their support of her. Interestingly, the stronger she became, the more support she picked up from other friends and family members.

As happens so often when people experience unconditional self-regard and move toward authenticity, she became confident, energized, and engaging. It wasn't long before her husband began to find her attractive. He began spending more and more time with her—supposedly because she was demanding it, but actually because he found her so much more enjoyable to be around.

I doubt that Julie could have taken the steps she did without her cheering section. Her therapy group modeled unconditional love for her, and in time she experienced it for herself. This gave her the huge boost she needed to confront the problems in her life.

■

YOU NEED TO EXPERIENCE THE CONSTANTLY RECURRING DYNAMIC

When you are lost, the *first thing you need to do is to become aware of your lostness.* You need to know that the person you have come to experience yourself as being is not the person you were meant to be. Whether it be a crisis or some "bottoming-out" event that brings you to this awareness, the process of starting over requires a conscious recognition of your plight.

Once you have acknowledged your lostness, your starting over—your rebirth—may seem virtually impossible. You are entangled in a web of emotional deals you have made with countless people, some as close as your parents or your spouse and some as distant as your boss or neighbor. These persons may appear to have a hold on you that seems impossible to break. Whatever they are giving you—usually some indication of your worth or value—may make it seem that you are a prisoner for life, that you will lose all of this approval if you fail to keep your end of the bargain. Your part of the deal, of course, is to let them define you, let them tell you what to think and feel.

So the *second thing you need to do is to become convinced that you can survive any consequence of breaking the bargain*—that you can handle the usual punishment, condemnation, or rejection from these people. You come to believe that if every person in your life were to stop caring for you, you would still have value, still be lovable, still be a person of great worth. This requires a powerful infusion into your life of unconditional positive regard. This dynamic assures you that your worth as a person is permanently established and that there is no need for you to worry that it can be taken away.

The fact is, the struggle to break free from the old agreements will be incredibly difficult. You will be mauled by frustrated old "allies," lured by old habits and addictions, and generally thwarted on every turn in your effort to get back "home." Therefore, your need to encounter unconditional positive regard will be tremendous. It will only be as you receive this dynamic from important others, and then believe it yourself, that you will be able to fight through the entanglements. It really helps if you can hear the dynamic explained all over again at least once a week and can regularly feel it working its way into dozens of conversations and real-life events. *Unconditional positive regard is the only thing that will make it possible for you to win the struggle.*

My clients often ask me what they should do about relationships that are based on conditions and stipulations, relationships in which they have dealt away pieces of their individuality for superficial positive regard. Should they abandon these old relationships and move on to newer, healthier ones? I encourage these people to prioritize their concerns. Their first concern, I believe, has to be their own rebirth process. Then they will want to help others in their effort to start over. But if another person has no interest in breaking out of the old ways and remains intent on pulling them back into the miserable emotional deals, I encourage them to move away from these relationships.

The more often you can encounter unconditional positive regard, the more likely it is that you can successfully complete your journey to authenticity and, ultimately, contentment. So I suggest that you pour your time and energy into those relationships characterized by unqualified acceptance and that you withdraw from those relationships in which this dynamic is missing.

The struggle to become whole again, to become centered, to be reborn, is always ferociously fought. You need all the help you can get. Encountering on a regular basis the dynamic that makes it all possible is a vital part of the rebirth process.

■

chapter seven

LET YOUR VALUES INFORM YOUR DECISIONS

☐Let's imagine that you are standing in the middle of your control booth and that you are concentrating on a decision that will greatly affect your life. You know that your two-part challenge is first to gather all your important data from every crucial source and second to evaluate that information and make the best decision possible. This is the way to authenticity.

One of the most vital pieces of data you will need to analyze relates to your values. A *value* is a principle you subscribe to—a principle that is nearly always valid.

You might think of values as a major part of your inner guidance system. They are your internal code—guidelines that point the way toward wise, dependable, trustworthy decisions. *If contentment hinges on being true to yourself, and if being true to yourself hinges on making wise choices moment by moment, then making wise choices hinges on your ability to clarify your values and allow them to exert substantive influence on your choosing.* We might say it the opposite way: If you want to jeopardize contentment, make frequent decisions that are contrary to your values.

Christy is twenty-eight years old and has never been married, though she would like to be someday if she could find someone who matches up well with her personality, goals, and beliefs. Todd is twenty-nine years old, and though he has had several serious relationships, he also has never married.

One Tuesday evening, Christy is obsessing about being lonely and is lamenting her recent lack of dates. Right on cue, Todd calls and asks her to go to a party with him on the following Saturday night. Christy likes Todd a lot. On the basis of everything she knows about him, she thinks he's the kind of man with whom she could build a long-term relationship. Todd tells her about the party, and it sounds like something she would thoroughly enjoy.

But here's the rub: For the last six months, Todd has been dating Monica, a college friend of Christy's. In fact, that's how Christy met Todd in the first place. Monica introduced them. To complicate things even further, Christy isn't sure that Todd and Monica have broken up. Monica has confided to Christy that they have been having problems for the last two months, but Christy also knows that her friend still has strong feelings for Todd.

So there is Christy's dilemma. She wants to go out with Todd, and he obviously wants to go out with her. But what about Monica?

Christy stands in her control booth, and she collects all the data. Everything is positive except for one principle that's extremely important to her: She knows it's wrong to violate the trust of another person—

especially a friend—and she knows that Monica would consider her going out with Todd to be a violation. She has to say no.

Christy explains her decision as fully as possible to Todd, and he doesn't offer any insight into his status with Monica that would cause her to reevaluate her choice. She is taking a big risk because she really likes Todd and knows she may never hear from him again. As she hangs up the phone, Christy is disappointed, but she is confident that she has made a wise decision that represents her deepest self.

■

VALUES COME IN ALL SHAPES AND SIZES

Every week, perhaps every day, you face decisions that will be influenced by your values. Should you be completely honest or shade the truth a little? Should you take the extra time to give a kind response or should you hurry on to make your appointment? Should you take your friend to the airport even though it's inconvenient or should you lie and say you have another commitment? How you answer these questions—how you respond to your inner guidance system—has a great deal to do with your ability to attain long-lasting, soul-satisfying contentment. Consider a few situations where values come into play:

PETER

Peter owns an apartment building that he is desperate to sell. He has an open listing with a real estate broker who shows the building to Herb, a very interested potential buyer. The next day, Peter gets a call from Herb.

"Peter, why don't we work out a deal between the two of us? If we leave your Realtor out of it, we can split whatever her commission would've been. I'm not sure I could afford the building otherwise, and besides, this way you won't have to fork over thousands of dollars to her. We'd both come out ahead!"

Peter is certainly intrigued by the idea, but he strongly believes in the value of complete honesty. His decision is made, even though it tears him apart to refuse Herb's offer.

MARCY

Marcy and Jackie used to be good friends before Jackie decided to cut her off. They still share the same group of friends, even though they hardly speak to each other anymore. Now Marcy has learned that Jackie was arrested for using drugs, something she's managed to keep most people from discovering. If this news got out, it would be extremely hurtful to Jackie.

Marcy thinks, *Maybe I'll just happen to mention the arrest to Jen, who can never keep a secret. She'll blab it to everyone else. Nobody will want anything to do with Jackie.*

But then she comes to her senses. She couldn't do this to someone—even to someone who is a *former* friend. One of Marcy's values is to remain totally free of gossip and behind-the-back tales. She will not spread rumors—period.

LINDA

Rob is about to ask Linda to marry him, and Linda knows it. She is wonderfully happy—she can't imagine a man she could love more.

But something has been nagging at her, something she has meant to talk with Rob about but just never got around to. She was bulimic for two years; she even had to spend a month at a treatment center to help her deal with the eating disorder.

Although she has overcome the problem, she's embarrassed to admit she ever struggled with bulimia. What would Rob think? Would he always wonder if she might fall back into the disorder? Would this revelation cause him to change his mind about marriage? She would be devastated if it did.

It would be so much easier just to avoid the subject, to sweep it under the rug. But Linda subscribes to the value of full disclosure and total integrity. She deeply believes that Rob deserves to know something this crucial about her life. Despite the fact that everything in her wants to compromise this value, she decides to share her secret.

■

VALUES SERVE AS AN ANCHOR, EVEN THOUGH WE MAY WANT TO COMPROMISE

Let me set the context one more time. If you want to be enduringly content, there is only one way to bring it about: You have to become an authentic person—that person you truly are. And there is only one way to become authentic: *You must take possession of your own control booth and make careful and competent choices at every point along the way.*

Competent choosing involves collecting all of the related data. Then you stand in the middle of all this data and make the best choice you can.

Among the data you need to collect are any relevant values that bear on the decision you need to make. *Relevant values* involve principles you espouse. You espouse these principles because they have proven to be valid over time and under a broad range of circumstances. Or perhaps you espouse them because they are part of an authority or faith system to which you have pledged yourself.

We often want to rethink our values in the middle of a decision. But one of the most useful aspects of values is that they serve as an anchor that we can trust when emotion runs high and time runs short. Consider the value of honesty, for instance. When we come to a high-emotion moment and we are asked a question, we will virtually always be best off if we are honest. But if you are like me, there are times when honesty seems detrimental to our welfare, and we begin to reason that this may be a good time to make an exception.

My wife and I were driving to the desert recently when I was pulled over for speeding. The speed limit on this long, relatively empty freeway near Palm Springs is seventy miles per hour, but virtually no one goes seventy. The California Highway Patrol officer said that at one point he had clocked me at eighty, and then he asked me how fast I thought I was going. Sometimes my brain takes a while to come up with a response, but not this time!

I remembered going nearly eighty a few miles back, but I honestly thought I was going seventy-three before he pulled me over. Then I remembered that my son-in-law had told me that if you are going even one mile over the limit, you are deemed guilty. All this was bouncing around my mind in the nanoseconds between that giant policeman's question and my mumbled answer.

"Seventy-three," I said plaintively.

"You *were* going seventy-three just before I pulled you over," he said, "but two miles back you were going eighty."

My value of honesty and my desire to be found innocent waged a fierce battle in less than a second. My brain compromised on seventy-three. Unfortunately, the officer operated under a different value system. I was cited for doing eighty in a seventy zone.

If I had been totally true to my value of honesty, I would have ended up far more content. I wish that I would have told the truth unequivocally: "Officer, I remember going nearly eighty a few miles back, but two or three minutes before you pulled me over I noticed that I was going seventy-three."

Obviously, the result would have been the same, but my trust in my own strength of character, and perhaps my wife's trust in me, would have been maximized. Contentment is often a function of how much you believe in your own high performance—especially when you are under pressure.

·

FIVE VALUES THAT MOST INFLUENCE MY DECISION MAKING

All of us have slightly different sets of values. We were raised by different people, and we may ascribe to different religious and societal codes. But I suspect that my five most crucial values may be similar to yours.

I recently listed all of my values, and I was startled by the number of them. In fact, I would encourage you to write down all the values you hold, values you believe to be consistently important to your thinking. Then select the five most important values in relation to your decision making. See how your list compares with mine.

FAIRNESS

I boil when anyone—myself or other people—is treated unfairly. Perhaps this is why I try so hard to be fair in my own decision making. This partially explains why I get so persnickety when I come to an intersection with a four-way stop. Every person in line from all four directions is asked to make one or more decisions, and at the center of these decisions is their level of fairness. Every driver must proceed only when his or her turn comes.

I get mad when someone comes flying up to the intersection, barely stops, and then pushes in front of others who were there first. This kind of decision making is selfish—and the principle of fairness doesn't come into play at all.

The value of fairness is relevant to so many of life's decisions. In a business partnership, every partner must carry his or her fair share of the load. The same is true, of course, in marriage. Child rearing calls for a fair distribution of labor. As a matter of fact, every encounter between two people brings the matter of fairness into consideration.

Figuring out what is fair can sometimes be terribly complex. For instance, my wife has worked a full-time, heavy-responsibility job since our youngest daughter left for college. She also carries far and away the most duties around our home. But before you leap to judgment that I am lazy and unfair, I must tell you that I, too, work extremely hard for our relationship, and I carry major responsibility in a host of other areas. Through the years, the fairness debate has never been too far from the surface for us. Fortunately for Marylyn and me, we now both feel that our relationship involves complete fairness. That's a big reason we enjoy each other so much.

When people are secure enough that they don't have to seek every little advantage for themselves, they are able to engage with others in relationships that create deep emotional trust. Show me a person who is genuinely fair in all her dealings, and I will show you a person whose life is almost sure to be interpersonally successful.

HONESTY

My dad was an honest man. He didn't cheat, and he didn't lie.

When I was seventeen years old and living in California, my friend Mel Rowan and I wanted to fly to New York to pick up a new car. We checked on airfares and discovered that a major airline was offering a special deal. If two members of the same family were flying together, one could fly at half price. So Mel and I asked my dad if he would buy the tickets for us and simply indicate that Mel was my brother. It would have saved us, and him, a significant amount of money.

His answer was not harsh, but it was immediate and final. No, he wouldn't do that. Even if no one discovered the deception, it wasn't honest. At the time, I considered him to be truthful to a fault. *What's the big deal?* I thought. *Mel and I are* practically *brothers.*

I no longer question that decision by my dad—or any of the thousands of decisions that demonstrated his total allegiance to honesty. His truthfulness has been highly influential throughout my life.

Still, should honesty be rigidly applied as a value? After all these years of conducting therapy with thousands of people, I have come to believe that truth telling is almost always vital to the development of strong relationships. Lies and deception drive a wedge between people and create turmoil for the one who tells them. There are some rare exceptions, of course. If I had been a citizen of Poland during the Second World War, I would have tried to hide as many of my Jewish friends as I could. And if the Nazi authorities had come to my door and asked if I was hiding any Jews, I would have lied.

Sometimes I may take honesty too far. When our daughters were growing up, they saddled me with the nickname of Dr. Blunt. I believed so deeply in telling the whole truth that when our girls asked what I thought of their new hairstyles, their outfits, or their essays, I would tell them exactly what I thought. Sometimes I should have been wiser and figured out that they really wanted encouragement and affirmation. That doesn't mean I would have lied—I just would not have told them *everything* I thought.

But when people make important decisions and are guided by their commitment to truthfulness, they are inevitably trustworthy. They won't cheat you, so you can rely on them. I am strongly persuaded that in close relationships, trust is at the center of everything good, and consistent honesty is the secret ingredient for multiplying and enlarging trust.

KINDNESS

Kindness is defined as the quality of showing sympathy, consideration, and helpfulness. This quality seems to have universal appeal. Cross-cultural studies show that kindness is at the top of the list of attributes potential marriage partners are looking for in a mate.

Let me give you an example of kindness. The lead secretary and office manager for the company I operate is a woman in her early thirties named Sue Braden. She has a hectic job, but I've noticed that she is exceedingly kind in all of her interactions. Some days we receive two to three hundred telephone calls from people who want to obtain my books, videotapes, audiocassettes, tests, or information about seminars. Sue treats every person as if they are more important than any other human being on earth. However busy she is, she listens carefully, sympathizes warmly, and responds immediately with efficiency and good humor. I never cease being impressed by her. At the center of her control booth, she must be surrounded by dozens of signs that say PEOPLE ARE PRECIOUS! TREAT THEM WITH KINDNESS.

What is so appealing about kindness? I believe the attraction relates to that fundamental motivation I referred to earlier. If we all want more than anything else to feel good about ourselves, we are overjoyed to encounter someone like Sue Braden. She makes us feel that we have incredible value.

It doesn't matter whether kindness comes from a friend or a stranger; it totally changes any interpersonal encounter. I know a man who works in a parking lot collection booth, and he contributes to my day by the way he relates to me. Kindness makes every relationship better. If you value this quality, you need to stay alert to its importance as your brain makes decisions in the interests of your authenticity—and your eventual contentment.

FREEDOM

I'm not talking here about the freedom we have to vote, to worship where we want, or to say whatever we want without fear of reprisal from the authorities—although those are incredible freedoms we should never take for granted. The freedom I'm referring to has to do with the ability to be completely yourself, to be released from shame, guilt, fear, or anything else that might prevent you from freely acting, speaking, and believing the way you want to act, speak, and believe.

When I make decisions that influence my life, my grandchildren, my friends, or my employees, I carefully consider this value of freedom. I can provide freedom for others only when I feel secure inside myself. When I'm uptight about my own value as a person, I become tempted to use all my power to dictate to others how they must be around me.

My grandchildren blossom and flourish when they discover in me someone who gives them maximum opportunity to express their uniqueness. If I closely attend to them and thoroughly enjoy them, if I let them know that their value to me is not determined by how perfect they are or how well they perform, they enjoy their time with me and taste a little bit of freedom. I need to maintain reasonable limits, of course, but it's surprising how seldom I have to reestablish boundaries when I'm inwardly secure and offering freedom.

For instance, I recently held a surprise birthday party for my wife. It was a fancy black-tie affair at a local hotel, and I invited twenty-seven of Marylyn's favorite people. A band played, we enjoyed a delicious dinner, and then we viewed a videotape I had put together that featured photos of Marylyn throughout her life.

As I was planning the party, it occurred to me that for this to be a perfect event for Marylyn, her nine grandchildren needed to be there. *But how will that work?* I thought. *Nine kids in such an elegant setting with all the adults?* Our daughters introduced the idea to their children, the oldest of whom is only seven, and they were excited. The little kids got all dressed up and came to the party for one hour. By limiting the time they were there, and by turning all our attention to them, we set them free to be fully themselves. They were the hit of the night. They overwhelmed Marylyn with their enthusiasm for her birthday celebration, and their freedom made it possible for them to express their incredible love for her.

As much as I can, I want people to be deeply authentic in relation to me. When persons are genuinely free, they are most likely to be authentic. When they are authentic, they are almost sure to be content. I simply love being around enduringly contented people.

GENEROSITY

Generosity may very well be my favorite value. I find nothing more attractive in others than generosity. This is such a noble virtue, and people who practice it in their decision making contribute magnificently to the lives of others.

I have witnessed some incredibly generous people up close. My dad freely shared his money. My mother was unusually generous with her love. My mother-in-law, Mary Younkman, was unbelievably generous to Marylyn and me during the first decade of our marriage when we were so financially needy.

Generosity doesn't always involve material things. My friend Nell Privett generously praises my ideas and my writing, and she makes me feel extremely good about myself. Nell is imbued with generosity, so she warmly shares her appreciation of me.

People like this bring generosity into play when they have a decision to make. It influences their choices and moves them more and more in the direction of authenticity because they believe so deeply in the long-term importance of this value.

■

THE IMPORTANCE OF VALUES IN DECISION MAKING

Values are crucial in the management of your data, in deciding how to be true to all the feelings, thoughts, and convictions you collect about any decision. Still, can a person's values ever get in the way of their authenticity? Can we hold so tightly to these time-tested principles that they lead us to be untrue to ourselves? I don't think so, but let me explain.

Imagine you receive an invitation to the wedding of a close friend's daughter. You don't know the bride-to-be very well, and you don't know her fiancé at all. Trying to determine your response, you project yourself ahead to the Saturday afternoon in question, and you envision yourself at the event. All kinds of thoughts and feelings flood your brain.

You think of how boring most weddings are, especially if you aren't well acquainted with the couple getting married. You think of the long reception afterward, all the strangers milling around you, the loud music, the endless snapping of photographs, and the catered food, which is probably not what you would order for yourself.

But you also think of how inspired you often feel at weddings, how the ceremony lifts your spirits and encourages a new commitment to your ideals. You think about some old friends who will be there, friends with whom you would like to spend time.

You are simply caught in the middle of your ambivalence—until a strong signal flashes across your brain. A value high on your list is "Do unto others as you would like others to do unto you." You suddenly imagine your daughter or son being married on that Saturday, your sending an invitation to this couple to attend, and their reply. You are delighted when they say yes, saddened when they decline. Your ambivalence gives way to clarity. You need to be at that wedding.

But are you being authentic? *It may be a close call, but if you attend closely to your most cherished values at times of decision, they will usually lead you in the direction of authenticity.* And this authenticity of yours will inevitably produce that quality we refer to as enduring contentment.

part three

LIVING THE AUTHENTIC LIFE

■

chapter eight

TEN CHARACTERISTICS OF AUTHENTIC PEOPLE

Because our society so heavily emphasizes externals—what we can see, touch, and taste—there is not much discussion in the media, at social gatherings, or even around family dinner tables about what it means to be internally authentic and genuine. Likewise, there is little dialogue about how to achieve a deep level of life satisfaction.

The lack of discourse on these topics leaves many people vague and unclear when it comes to the issues of contentment and authenticity. We're left with many questions: How do we know—exactly—what it means to be authentic? How can we recognize this quality in others and in ourselves? What are the internal ingredients that will lead to contentment?

If you agree with me that contentment is contingent upon being authentic, then we would be wise to know precisely what authenticity looks like. I believe ten characteristics are present in authentic people. These are, in fact, the very threads that weave together the fabric of enduring contentment.

■

1. AUTHENTIC PEOPLE LIVE
IN THE PRESENT

It's all too easy to live life in the future or in the past. When this happens we relive the glories and missed opportunities of years gone by or we yearn for the better days ahead. In either case, we fail to experience life as it happens. You know someone, I'm sure, who always talks about days of old ("Remember when our college football team played for the championship and I scored the winning touchdown?") or how life will improve in the future ("When the kids are grown and out of the house, I'll be free to do what I want"). There's nothing wrong with having fond memories of the past and aspirations for the future, but when they dominate your life focus, you miss the joy and richness of life *as it unfolds*.

The work of Professor Carl Rogers, one of the most influential American-born psychologists, has affected my life enormously. I first learned the power of "living in the now" from Rogers. His therapeutic approach emphasized the present because he was convinced that life is more fulfilling and rewarding when we focus on *this moment*.

As a young psychology instructor, I carried the Rogerian message into every graduate class I taught. I told my students that life is most exciting and satisfying when we are free to encounter it at its freshest and richest point—right now.

But it was years later—after I had become the dean of the graduate school where I taught—that Professor Thomas Oden of Drew University helped me to understand more precisely the relationship between being present in the moment and being in tune with the deepest and most central parts of one's inner self. Dr. Oden recognized that primarily anxiety and guilt keep us from focusing on the present. He argued persuasively that anxiety almost always relates to the future. When we doubt our ability to handle prospective challenges, our anxiety increases. Consequently, we devote more thought and energy to these matters. We worry, fret, and stew over what might happen. And the more we focus on the future, the less available we are to the present.

Similarly, Professor Oden said guilt almost always has to do with the past—mistakes we made, problems we didn't handle wisely, projects we left undone, people we let down. The guilt we experience about past events causes us to continue attending to them, and this preoccupation also shifts our focus away from the present.

My experience with the Christian faith made Dr. Oden's principles for dealing with guilt and anxiety extremely helpful. Hope for the future is built on faith in God, he reasoned. Our confidence in God is always based on past events—how He has proved Himself reliable and consistent in our lives and throughout history. *When faith is well established, we become convinced that He will guide us and help us through any future challenge.* This assurance, built on faith, frees us from anxiety—and allows us to remain in the present.

A similar principle applies to guilt. *The promise of forgiveness enables us to release our guilt.* When we truly experience forgiveness, we can let go of our concern about the mismanagement of past events. We are no longer bound by the past and are instead liberated to live fully in the present.

What's more, as we endeavor to live in a way that is true to our inner thoughts, convictions, and inclinations, we will increase the likelihood of living in the present. We will manage daily events and problems in a more thorough and thoughtful way, thereby creating less guilt. As we experience our ability to work wisely through each new challenge, we become more and more assured that we will be able to handle whatever our future holds. *Our mastery of the present reduces our anxiety about the future and frees us to focus even more on the immediate.* This is the powerful momentum that emotional health tends to create for us. On the other hand, when forgiveness and hope are absent for us, the same powerful momentum is equally likely *in reverse.*

■

2. AUTHENTIC PEOPLE ARE FREE OF FEAR

When you are in complete harmony with your internal world, there is nothing to be anxious about. You have nothing to hide, and you can freely be yourself. If you are true to yourself in every moment, confidently living out who you are, there is no fear of rejection from others, no fear of being "caught" doing something you would feel bad about, no fear of having to measure up to standards others impose on you.

Authentic people need not worry about being inconsistent or duplicitous, having to act one way around some people and another way around others. There is no pretense to maintain or image to keep polished. There is no apprehension about how you respond to other people—or how they respond to you.

Nothing is so liberating as simply being yourself as fully as you know how. It was Søren Kierkegaard who made the ultimate goal famous: "To be that self which one truly is."

When your goal is to stand in the middle of all your data and make a choice about who you are in that moment, you have no need for fear.

■

3. AUTHENTIC PEOPLE ARE NOT JUDGMENTAL

We cannot develop authenticity unless we have unconditional positive regard for ourselves. As we discussed in Chapter 6, positive self-regard means accepting yourself fully for who you are, appreciating your unique makeup and design, having a high degree of self-respect, and basing your sense of worth or value not on achievement or performance, but on intrinsic value established at the outset.

People who have nonjudgmental attitudes are almost always authentic. This doesn't mean, of course, that they make no judgments; after all, careful assessments play a major role in the contented life. But it does mean that while they're judging issues and problems, they always offer positive regard to others. They evaluate thoughts and opinions—even ones they disagree with—while treating those who hold them with complete respect and dignity. They don't have to be better than someone else is. They don't have to satisfy someone else's criteria to feel good about themselves. They are in touch with the deepest and best of their internal world. That's why they can be so generous in their attributions of worth to others.

When you encounter people like this, stay around them as much as you can. They will help you in your quest to become a person of integrity and wholeness.

■

4. AUTHENTIC PEOPLE GENUINELY APPRECIATE THEMSELVES

People who appreciate themselves are self-confident and secure, not cocky and conceited. The difference is easy to identify over time. When a person is conceited, he acts defensive, competitive, arrogant, and perhaps even hostile. But a person who is truly self-confident exudes a sense of inner security, assurance, and composure.

Appreciating yourself in a healthy way has everything to do with a proper self-concept. When I talk with someone, four clues tell me if the person has a healthy self-concept or not:

1. *Pace of interaction.* I discover very quickly when a person is unsure of himself—he talks too much or too little, too fast or too slow. He leaves no room for me to be involved in the conversation, or he expects me to carry the entire conversation. He and I are not in harmony with each other, and that's often a strong indication that he's not in harmony with himself.

2. *Defensiveness.* If the person seems overly sensitive, easily threatened or hurt, or determined to win me over to his point of view, I know he feels insecure. This type of defensiveness is usually a

sign that he perceives his self-worth to be in question and that he feels a pressing need to convince me that he is okay.

3. *Self-image.* People who have a well-developed self-image are almost always positive and kind when talking about themselves. They may point out their inconsistencies and shortcomings but usually in the context of a broader and more favorable view of themselves. This benevolent attitude also holds true when they are talking about other people.

4. *Anger management.* A person with a well-developed self-concept will know how to manage anger in a positive way. Even when the individual has a lot of anger, it isn't explosive and damaging to relationships. It can be channeled appropriately and used as a constructive resource.

Developing a healthy self-concept and appreciating yourself are signs that you've done a lot of inner work, that you've become comfortable with who you are, and that you are seeking wholeness. And all of these components are fundamental to contentment.

■

5. AUTHENTIC PEOPLE HUNGER FOR THE TRUTH

I have known Debby for several years. She has been in my Monday-night therapy group longer than any other person has. The truth is, she doesn't need to come anymore. For months I have told her that she's one of the healthiest people I know, but she keeps coming because this group has become her family. Besides, she continues to grow.

Through the years of Debby's therapy, I have watched one of her qualities develop tremendously—she may have more respect for the truth than any other person I know. Whereas some people might shade the truth to get out of an awkward situation or to cast themselves in a better light, Debby demonstrates integrity and precision in everything she says. Whereas some people might betray a hint of pretension or phoniness, Debby is unfailingly forthright and candid. There is not a whiff of falsehood about her.

When you ask Debby a tough question—one that has the potential of making her look "bad"—she takes plenty of time to formulate her answer. She may ask a few questions of her own, and then she may collect more information from inside herself—from her thoughts and feelings. Then she delivers her answer. She does a thorough job of collecting the data. Time after time, she amazes me! Her answers are not only insightful, but they seem so exact and unequivocal as well.

I guarantee that when you encounter these rare people who are dedicated to the whole truth in any given moment, you will note that they are in touch with their deepest and most profound inner parts. They are being fully themselves, and this is what authenticity is all about.

■

6. AUTHENTIC PEOPLE ARE ADAPTABLE AND FLEXIBLE

People who have learned to be authentic are not annoyed and upset by every little change that comes along. They aren't so rigid and unbending that the inevitable twists and turns of life rock their world.

For instance, I frequently tell couples that one of the most important marital attributes is adaptability. If two people are married for many
years, each of them will go through countless changes that will take
them in new directions. For the marriage to stay vital, both partners
will need to adapt to all the changes individually and as a couple. Only
people who are sufficiently secure within themselves can achieve this
kind of adaptability.

Authentic people have what I call *healthy adaptability*—the kind
that is free from resentment and feelings of abuse. They are so inwardly
secure and sure of who they are that change for the benefit of a valued
relationship will seem relatively easy. On the other hand, someone who
is insecure and out of sync will tend to be defensive and angry when
confronted by the need for change. *Survival in life requires constant adap-
tation, and those who master the skill are headed toward contentment.*

■

7. AUTHENTIC PEOPLE HAVE A STRONG SENSE OF GRATITUDE

I recently had lunch with Dr. Lewis Smedes, a professor of social
ethics and the author of many acclaimed books. I asked him to comment
on the secret of attaining contentment. He thought for a long while and
finally said: "*Gratitude* is at the very heart of contentment. My sense of
satisfaction in life springs from the feeling of gratitude. I have never
met a truly thankful, appreciative person who was not happy. So close
are gratitude and contentment that I would equate them."

Think of that! This brilliant thinker and social ethicist says that
when you are grateful you are almost sure to be enduringly content.

At the heart of this principle are two aspects fundamental to contentment:

- *Gratitude means appreciating what you have, not yearning for what you don't have.* Being thankful to God for all that we've been given—instead of complaining about what we're missing—is at the core of well-being.
- *Gratitude is the recognition that we cannot do well in life on our own.* We need people to invest in our lives, nurture us, and help us along at critical points.

I often think of the monumental role my mother played in my life. She was a simple woman who loved me with every fiber of her being. Though she graduated from only the eighth grade, she taught me things about life that none of my graduate school professors even thought to mention. She demonstrated a fierce loyalty to those she loved, a sensitivity to all people's feelings, and an appreciation for the practical over the theoretical. I am a far happier man when I recall all that my mother gave so generously to me.

When gratitude dominates our thoughts and feelings, we are sure to be deeply satisfied. Dr. Smedes is right: Gratitude and contentment are so closely intertwined that we can't have one without the other.

■

8. AUTHENTIC PEOPLE LOVE TO LAUGH AND ARE LIGHTHEARTED

Norman Cousins highlighted so powerfully the therapeutic effects of laughter. In his classic book *Anatomy of an Illness,* Professor Cousins related the poignant story of his personal victory over cancer—a victory that involved listening to numerous comedy tapes and viewing hilarious old movies that made him laugh unendingly.

In addition to being therapeutic for the body, laughter and lightheartedness also signify inner wholeness and tranquillity. I think of the Proverb that says, "A merry heart does good, like medicine, / But a broken spirit dries the bones" (17:22). Of course, not everyone who laughs frequently and freely is perfectly centered in his inner world, but I suspect that any person who lives authentically is almost certainly able to laugh and see the lighter side of life. *A buoyant and jovial spirit is a by-product of authenticity.*

My older sister, Ferne, regularly calls to tell me a joke and to laugh with me. The freedom with which we laugh together tells me how the two of us are doing. There is something so freeing and lifting about insyncness that can only be expressed through laughter and lightheartedness.

When it comes to wholeness and laughter, our middle daughter, Luann, has always been fascinating to study. I don't know anyone else as popular with a greater diversity of people, and a major part of Luann's attractiveness is her affability and frequent laughter.

Luann has a wit that has grown magnificently over time, but it isn't her own wit I find so interesting. Rather, it is her ability to enjoy a moment, her appreciation of other people's witty remarks, and her special ability to see the interplay of words and ideas that leads to humor. This wonderful gift makes her such an enjoyable partner in conversation, such a transmitter of good feelings to anyone involved, that people love to be around her.

How is Luann able to enjoy, and help others enjoy, so many moments? She has been endowed with a bright mind and positive attitude, but far more important is her security in who she is, her centeredness, her ability to express herself freely. And for her that means laughing in a way that makes those involved feel good about themselves.

Study the people you know who are enduringly content. See if these people don't exude winsome spirits and fun-loving attitudes. See if there aren't twinkles in their eyes and perpetual grins on their faces. See if you don't find yourself getting carried along by their lightheartedness and frequent laughter.

■

9. AUTHENTIC PEOPLE EXHIBIT A HIGH DEGREE OF DIGNITY

Lee Edward Travis, the dean of the school at which I first taught, was the most outstanding human being I have ever known. Dr. Travis was a pioneer psychologist in America who published some two-hundred and fifty articles and books. But his scholarship had little to do with my admiration for him. His greatness in my eyes had to do with his authenticity—an authenticity that showed itself clearly in an unusual dignity. Dr. Travis had spent considerable time learning about himself and discovering his inner world.

I well remember my first meeting—which occurred over the telephone—with this world-renowned scholar and leader. I was a graduate student at The University of Chicago, and I was terribly nervous about talking to Dr. Travis. Within two sentences, he put me totally at ease. He made me feel like I was incredibly important. I liked him instantly, and he immediately became a mentor and a kind of hero for me.

I wanted to learn his secret for relating to people. How did he make such a powerful impression on me and on others—an impression that only grew through the years? It had everything to do with the magnificently authentic and dignified way with which he presented himself. Perhaps it had even more to do with the respect he accorded me.

Authentic people treat everyone—themselves included—with the utmost respect. They can do this, I think, because they are sure and confident about who they are. Whatever you tell them will never have ultimate power over them, so they don't become anxious and frantic that you are going to push an agenda or apply pressure to get your way. They engage in two straightforward and highly practiced acts—collecting information and making decisions.

Dignity involves a peaceful spirit, and a *peaceful spirit* is the result of one experience after another in which you are attentive to your inner world and make choices that show respect for yourself at every point along the way.

■

10. AUTHENTIC PEOPLE SLEEP WELL

There is something highly diagnostic about peaceful sleep. Show me a person who sleeps unusually well, and I will show you a person who is fundamentally in harmony with his or her world.

Let me reason in reverse for a minute. Four factors usually contribute to sleep problems:

1. **You may be under a lot of stress.** Perhaps you're overworked and feeling pressure. Obviously, this may happen now and then to the most authentic person in the world, but if you frequently sleep poorly because you are stressed from overwork, it is a clear sign that you're serving a false master, that you're trying way too hard to establish your worth through achievement.

2. **You may drink too much alcohol.** Millions of Americans drink large amounts of alcohol in an effort to feel better about themselves. Even though alcohol may give you temporary relief, it almost always exacts a high price for its momentary value—a price that often includes the loss of peaceful sleep. Many people falsely believe that drinking alcohol will ensure a good night's sleep. Although feeling relaxed may help you fall asleep initially, alcohol actually makes deep sleep almost impossible.

3. **You may be overweight or may not be getting enough exercise.** Fifty million Americans weigh significantly more than they should, and it's time that we begin explaining what this self-sabotaging behavior is all about. It frequently indicates a lack of "internal friendship." That is, many people do not value themselves enough to make healthy living a priority. This lack of internal friendship is close to what I mean by being out of sync with your deepest and most central inner self.

4. **You may be anxious or worried.** There are myriad things to worry about—finances, relationships, car problems, deadlines—

and unless we deal with these in a healthy and authentic way, we will suffer the consequences.

The point is, if you consistently fail to sleep well, it's likely that one of these four factors is to blame. And if any of these factors applies to you, it's also likely to signal a deficit in authenticity. When you stay true to yourself, when you manage each moment as it comes your way, you can't live life any better. This kind of life management prepares you for the relaxation that is required for deep and peaceful sleep.

■

THESE TEN CHARACTERISTICS ARE THE CRUCIAL INDICATORS

If you want to find out about your own authenticity and in-sync-ness—or someone else's—look for the preceding ten characteristics. It's almost unbelievable how reliably they indicate emotional health. When you are internally in harmony with yourself, everything else about your life will suddenly get better.

I haven't sugarcoated the process of being authentic. Throughout this book, I have said it takes great courage and perseverance to be true to yourself and in sync every moment. And frankly, many people lack the courage and tenacity required to achieve authenticity. However, if you can see the task through, if you can complete the mission, you will experience a richness and satisfaction in life that most people can only dream about.

chapter nine

■

ROADBLOCKS TO AUTHENTICITY

☐My friend Erik makes no pretense about trying to become authentic. In fact, he subtly makes fun of the idea. He reminds me of Mordred, the illegitimate son of King Arthur in *Camelot*. Mordred sneers at what he calls the "seven deadly virtues," to which he hasn't the slightest attraction. Erik is like this when it comes to authenticity. He seems to believe that authenticity would get him nowhere.

I encounter scores of "Eriks" in the world, people for whom even the idea of authenticity seems irrelevant. If you question them persistently, you discover their bottom-line conclusion: Authenticity is confusing, overly demanding, unnatural, and not worth the supreme effort it requires. Sometimes these people have a faint understanding of the tragic price of their inauthenticity—that they will never know the rich contentment and peace that always accompany authenticity—but they've given up caring. They actively pursue other goals (or no goals at all).

In my experience, a vast majority of North Americans are not in the least authentic! Having encountered one roadblock to authenticity after another, they became discouraged, and a pursuit of momentary happiness dominates their lives. Authenticity becomes a viable alternative for them only when they totally bottom out, when they suffer a horrible setback of some kind, or when their families are torn apart by dissension.

I have often agonized about why so many people are unsuccessful in becoming authentic and have questioned dozens of individuals like this. I've discovered eight fundamental obstacles to achieving authenticity—reasons and excuses people have adopted to remain inauthentic.

■

1. THEY SIMPLY DON'T KNOW HOW TO BE AUTHENTIC

"Do you know what it means to be authentic?" I asked Erik.

He answered without a moment's hesitation. "I think it means to be the person you really are, but I don't know much about it beyond that."

Although I was eager to find out why he seemed so confidently inauthentic, I tried not to aggravate him with too many questions.

"I was totally inauthentic during many of my early years," I confessed to him, "and frankly, during that time, I didn't think about anything but pleasing others. I didn't consider how important it was to be true to myself."

"Yeah, I can relate. I don't think about that either," he said. It was clear he was eager to have this conversation move in a different direction.

But there was more I wanted to find out about Erik's perspective. "If you actually *wanted* to be the person you really are, would you know how to go about doing it?"

For the first time, Erik seemed to sift through his thoughts for a few seconds.

"You got me on that one, Neil. I guess I wouldn't have the slightest idea!"

I wasn't trying to *get* him, but his response certainly reinforced one of my suspicions: Most people simply have no idea of how to be authentic. Unawareness in this area is the number one reason people in North America trudge through their inauthentic lives.

Frequently, this is because parents don't teach their children the ways of authenticity. Granted, the task of raising children to operate from the center of their control booths requires unusual health and sophistication on the part of parents. It's far easier to make puppets out of children and simply run their lives for them.

I have known many parents who systematically kept their children totally naive when it came to decision making and authenticity. I remember one little girl, Sondra, whose mother, Vicky, worked in an office close to mine. For nearly three years, Vicky brought her daughter to work every day, and I had many opportunities to observe her style of parenting.

Instead of helping Sondra learn how to make good decisions, Vicky simply let her do whatever she felt like doing whenever she felt like doing it. If Sondra ran noisily down the hall, Vicky dutifully followed close behind. When Sondra colored in valuable books in our waiting rooms, Vicky mildly and ineffectively scolded her. If Sondra scampered off before her new diaper was secured, Vicky resorted to pleading and chasing.

Sondra's body and mind operated on automatic pilot, which in this case was pure impulse. And over those three years of watching this little girl, I saw no signs of developmental progress in the area of decision making, probably because her mother consciously or unconsciously submitted to the little girl's every whim and urge.

There are all kinds of obstacles to authenticity, but one of the clearest and saddest is that a person has never learned the fine art of careful and responsible decision making and now hasn't the slightest idea of how to become authentic.

■

2. THEY KNOW BEING AUTHENTIC REQUIRES HARD WORK

The lifestyle that results in momentary happiness surges is far less demanding than what is required for deep and enduring contentment. *Happiness is all about what is outside you; contentment has to do with matters that are much more internal.*

All you have to do to be momentarily happy is to be in the right place at the right time, pay your money, and get ready to be entertained or thrilled or acted upon in one way or another. It's not hard, but what you get from it doesn't last long either. And eventually, of course, you begin to see how empty it all is. Before your very eyes, these happiness surges turn to vapor and then to smoke and then to smelly, invisible air.

The kind of authenticity that leads to contentment requires you to activate your brain and move inside this consciousness. Then, like a video camera, you have to turn your "lens" toward every relevant aspect of your life—both inside and outside. Next, you do something incredibly unique—you stand in the middle of all this *informed consciousness* and you make critical decisions. These decisions require an enormous amount of *conscious focus*. You have to hold this focus until you have made whatever choice is required of you. This requires strong mental discipline.

Let me illustrate how much more difficult it is to be authentic than it is to take the easy road of superficiality. Imagine that you have a Saturday with nothing to do. But then at nine, your friend Pat calls and suggests breakfast at a nearby café—Pat's favorite. Without giving it much thought, you say yes. You take a quick shower, put on some casual clothes, meet Pat at the restaurant, eat the usual, talk for a while, and then take off to do some errands. You do them haphazardly without a plan. After that, you head home, watch a game on television, grab a snack, and take a nap.

You may well ask if this six- or seven-hour stretch illustrates an authentic or inauthentic lifestyle. The correct answer is neither. What you do in your life does not necessarily determine whether you are living authentically or not. Authenticity has to do with whether your actions result from your choosing, oppose your choosing, or have nothing at all to do with your choosing. If you woke up on that particular Saturday thinking that you just wanted to relax and enjoy a day of total freedom, then the way you spent your day may have been completely authentic.

If, on the other hand, you had a long list of important things to get done, and you wasted all those hours, that's a likely indication of inauthenticity. Clearly, you violated your own choices, you weren't the person you wanted to be, and your degree of contentment was probably zero.

It is far more taxing to stay with your consciousness, move the video camera of your mind around and take in all the important factors about your living, and make thoughtful decisions from moment to moment. It is significantly easier to be pulled by outside events.

■

3. THEY ARE AFRAID AUTHENTICITY WILL LEAD TO SELF-CENTERED INDIVIDUALISM

Read this note from a person who listened to me talk about the need for authenticity:

Dear Dr. Warren,

When I heard you talk last week about authenticity, I felt inspired. But when I told my roommate about your approach, she said that it sounds so individualistic—like every person is going to be looking out for number one. If everyone were to stand in the middle of their own control booth, as you recommend, won't it just be every person for himself? Won't we all become unbelievably self-centered and selfish?

I get excited when people read my books or listen to my talks and then write me to discuss the material further. I know they're taking me seriously. Mind you, I think this woman's analysis of authenticity is dead wrong, but by expressing her concerns, she gives me another chance to clarify my ideas.

Authenticity, as you know by now, requires that you listen to *all* the input that may be involved with any decision you make. So the letter writer is worried that people will not give proper attention to the part of their data that relates to the wishes and concerns of others. She fears that people will make decisions based only on their own wishes, selfish ambitions, and individualistic goals.

This concern is well taken. To the degree that a person's self-concept is inadequately formed, and to the degree that a person's emotional health is deficient, that person's decisions might be overly self-seeking and self-protective. But when people become truly free to make uncluttered decisions based on all their relevant data, this is not the case. *Authentic people take all their data into consideration.* They treat other people's thoughts and wishes seriously and thoughtfully, because they know that what others need and want is important to their making a good decision.

Sometimes concern about authenticity comes from persons who are fearful of losing their control over the decision-making operation of another person. For instance, if an employer wants to maintain his control over the decision making of his employees, he may withhold vital information from them. When questioned, he will defend himself on the grounds that the employees are "probably not able" to make an unselfish decision.

Churches throughout history have been known to do the same thing. Wanting to keep their members under control, they have refused to allow members to look at important documents that might cause them to make decisions that would not be in the church's best inter-ests. Churches have argued that these members are "probably not able" to make wise and unselfish decisions.

I deeply believe that every individual, or group of individuals, deserves the opportunity to make decisions on the basis of all their data. When people criticize the ability of others to do this in a competent and unselfish manner, I am immediately suspicious.

I have watched thousands of persons in action, and I am convinced that those who are set free by unconditional positive regard are not essentially selfish. Far from it. People are essentially selfish when they are prisoners of some external force that is attempting to own and con-trol them. This selfishness is rooted in their fundamental anger result-ing from being blocked out of their own control booth.

■

4. THEY FEAR THEY'LL BECOME INCONSISTENT

"Left to themselves, individuals are enormously erratic." Thus, the argument goes, if we encourage people to be true to themselves and make regular decisions about the issues at hand, they will create the chaos that comes from inconsistency. In other words, someone who becomes authentic at forty might disregard all the decisions and com-mitments he made at twenty. In his newfound state of inner harmony, he may see the error of his earlier pledges and assessments.

Specifically, what if a woman marries a man when they are both in their mid-twenties? Then when she is forty, if given another oppor-tunity to make a decision about her marriage, she may choose to leave this man to whom she pledged her lifetime love only fifteen years earlier. Isn't this the kind of inconsistency you should expect?

Actually, I don't think this happens very often, although obviously it is a possibility. Judging from my experience, most persons who stay rooted in an authentic decision-making mode remain incredibly consistent in their fundamental attachments over time. The issue, however, is sometimes complex, and much of the complexity revolves around the degree of authenticity that characterized the original choice. For instance, if a woman makes a superficial decision to get married, and if her decision was essentially a poor one that failed to take into consideration crucial principles for wise mate selection, she is indeed in real danger if she later reaches a more mature developmental stage and revisits her earlier commitment.

There are certainly no guarantees that all the previous commitments, however wise or unwise they may have been, will be "remade" in the life of a person who becomes more authentic later. But take a look at the alternative. The person could remain oblivious. In an effort to safeguard all past commitments, he could refuse to consider his inner state, stay away from his control booth, and defend against any new appraisal of his current data picture.

Doing so may preserve the status quo, but the unexamined life seldom leads to authenticity. Contentment becomes virtually impossible. If the person slavishly maintains every former decision, the emptiness and frustration that accompany this imprisonment will become impossible to endure.

Don't get me wrong. I don't want to jeopardize sacred commitments that were made at an earlier time in a person's life. And I know that all past decisions are vulnerable to change under new circumstances. When you begin to live your life one day at a time, there is always a sense of threat to the old choices. But I strongly believe that the way to deal with this threat is by looking squarely at the truth as it exists currently. The continuity that maintains the former commitments are the values and principles that have been adopted, not the act of hiding one's eyes from what is true.

For instance, if a man and a woman committed themselves to each other many years ago, this commitment needs to be kept current year by year to stay strong and effective. If they discover that they would no longer make the same decision about each other, they need to devote themselves to reshaping their relationship so that is becomes newly satisfying and fulfilling. It is their commitment to the values of marital and family durability that holds them together during the time when they would otherwise scuttle their relationship.

But imagine how sick this relationship would become if they refused to look at their marriage. In the interests of preserving their union, they might allow it to be seriously eroded from the inside.

Good decision makers place tremendous emphasis on values. These values are the connective strands that hold them steady when circumstances change and the storms come. When people can look squarely at the truth about anything, they are in a position to bring their will to bear on it. Values give direction to their willful intervention.

I deeply believe that inconsistency—especially in relation to the more sacred matters of life—is for authentic people reduced to a fraction of what it is for individuals who are less centered in their decision making. On every level of human interaction, I have come to deeply trust the judgments of authentic people. They go right to their centers, explore every shred of truth, carefully choose their "presiding" values, and make decisions that are designed to be satisfying over the long term for all involved.

■

5. THEY FEAR THAT AUTHENTICITY WILL LEAD TO IMPULSIVENESS

I encourage every person to plant themselves at the center of their control booth and continually make decisions that affect their actions and their attitudes. If a person is encouraged to remain open to the possibility that a new decision is a better one, and that new information acquired later may lead to a change in the decision, then it might *appear* that the person is being impulsive.

The human task has become *so* complex! I am reminded of Harvard Professor Robert Kegan's insightful 1994 book, *In Over Our Heads*, in which he argues that the demanding events of life have placed neurological overloads on the structures of our brains.

I see this most frequently in mate selection. We now believe that there are as many as fifteen hundred dimensions related to the choosing of a marital partner for life. On each of these dimensions a person has an *optimal band* within which they would like the corresponding quality of their mate to fall. An easy example is height. Each person wishes for a mate whose height is within certain boundaries. When a prospective person walks up, your brain is assessing their height and comparing it with your own preferences.

Now multiply this single dimension of height by fifteen hundred, and you begin to see how incredibly complex mate selection is. And while this is a uniquely important and complex challenge, there are dozens of other similarly demanding challenges in this many-sided, fast-paced world in which we live. We could name them endlessly—how best to relate to the three persons "above" you who will determine your career future, how best to deal with the thirty-six persons "below" you whose future you will determine, how best to handle your stepson who at fourteen is already in deep trouble at school, doesn't like you very much, and is making all kinds of threats to your spouse.

Here's the point: Never has there been a society more demanding of reflective cognition than this one. We need to utilize all the power of the 2 billion-megabyte computer that we refer to as our brain. It is crucial that we not act on reflex. Too much hangs in the balance.

I strongly encourage people to make the best decision they can in every moment. I define as the *best decision* one that takes into consideration current, up-to-the-minute data, which may be different data from what was available at a previous time. Since new data may be factored in later, some decisions may seem to be sudden, as if they are impulsive. And sometimes they will appear to be reversals of prior decisions.

But I argue that *an authentic person does not make impulsive decisions.* After all, impulsive decisions are those in which *impulse* is dominant. The impulses are more likely to involve only partial data collection and therefore will be misguided. These are the choices that more often are made by a person who is not in charge of his decision-making ability and who is less able to consider all his data before a decision is made.

I believe that authenticity involves a full and free examination of all the data available, which is the opposite of impulsiveness. Moreover, the final decision of an authentic person will be one in which all of these data are taken carefully into consideration. This is highly likely to result in decisions that are stable over time. To the degree that data tends to remain consistent, decisions will tend to do the same.

■

6. THEY FEAR THEY'LL BECOME EMOTIONALLY AND INTELLECTUALLY LAZY

One time I invited my skeptical friend Erik to hear me talk on the link between authenticity and contentment. Afterward he said, "So, Neil, you're saying that becoming authentic will almost surely lead to contentment."

"I'm glad you were listening," I chided him. "That's exactly right."

"Then that convinces me that I never want to become authentic."

"Why's that? I'm not tracking with you."

"Well," Erik explained, "it seems to me that people who become content will just rest on their laurels. I mean, think about all the movers and shakers, the people who really make things happen. They seem to have a restless energy. If they were to become content, they would prob-ably also become complacent."

This roadblock always seems logical on the surface. At the heart of this issue is what motivates a person (or what reduces a person's moti-vation).

Most Americans seem to believe that people perform more efficiently and energetically if you keep them at least slightly dissatisfied. If you allow them to experience contentment, the argument goes, they will lose their competitive drive and will become lazy.

It's critical to distinguish between peacefulness and laziness. *Persons who are peaceful are not externally needy.* That is, they do not look to external sources to provide peace and well-being. This may be bad news for those people who want to control them, but it is great news to those who have already achieved this peacefulness.

For instance, the mother who wants her child to be needy of her because this makes her feel important and in control may not wish for the child to find internal peace. The child's very neediness gives the mother a deep sense of importance, of having a purpose and a place.

Of course, what I would say to this mother is that she must not base her own fulfillment on the neediness of her child. This will inevitably fail to satisfy her. All mothers and fathers are good parents only to the extent that they are fundamentally healthy and to the degree that their health is based on authenticity. When parents discover this basic form of emotional health, they can set their children free to be fulfilled, to be independently peaceful, and to grow well beyond their neediness.

Contented people are anything but lazy. On the whole, I believe they are more productive and prolific because they make wise choices that keep them on track and moving forward. Inauthentic people often fritter away time and energy managing all the emotional clutter in their lives and doing things to please others. For contented people, the absence of a frantic pace and pressurized schedule enables them to concentrate on tasks and goals that are truly important. As a matter of fact, these people usually experience a massive release of energy and creativity, which they use in constructive ways to change both their own lives and the lives of people around them.

I know a woman who is clearly one of the most authentic persons I have ever met, and there is not a lazy bone in her body. Edith Munger's difficult childhood no doubt prompted her to do a lot of internal work that contributed significantly to her eventual authenticity. And her unusual level of authenticity is matched by her endless service to others.

Edith is a psychologist who got her Ph.D. at an age when many of her peers were contemplating retirement. Her reason for waiting? She was raising two daughters, serving as the wife to one of the best-known Presbyterian pastors in America, and quietly making up for lost time in pursuing her education. Through all the demands of professional and family roles, Edith has acted out of her internal control booth, collected her data, made her decisions, lived courageously, and ended up influencing hundreds of lives.

I didn't know Edith personally until she became a doctoral student at the graduate school of psychology where I taught. Since then, I have met countless persons who knew her in earlier years. They all tell the same story about her. She was able to build a great marriage and be an excellent mother while maintaining her authenticity. And through it all, she found enormous joy in serving others while studying, growing, and constantly exercising her keen mind.

More than anything else, I want you to know that her level of contentment seems to only *increase* her commitment to pursue her goals wholeheartedly. On a laziness scale, she fails to register. She makes my point better than anyone else I know does. She is authentic, and she is supercharged with life and energy.

■

7. THEY KNOW IT WILL BE TOUGH TO STOP PLEASING EVERYONE

If momentary happiness is our only goal, we take a giant step toward it by making sure all the important people in our lives approve of who we are, what we stand for, and what we do. Conversely, the quest for authenticity will almost certainly mean we will not please everyone. *When we make careful decisions based on our true inner state, we will sometimes choose to be different from what others would like.* They may end up disgruntled with us and thoroughly unaccepting. This is one of the reasons we often surrender our authenticity. Rather than displeasing crucial people, we would rather adopt a false self.

For several months, I worked with a young woman named Chris, who had misgivings about her fiancé, Lamar, and was thinking about breaking off their engagement. Chris's parents loved Lamar and thought he would be a great son-in-law. Her mother had already planned most of the wedding and had made some nonrefundable deposits.

Chris knew her parents would be shocked and angry if she decided not to follow through with the wedding. This caused her anxiety to skyrocket because her parents were extremely important to her, and she was sincerely grateful for their involvement in her life. Sometimes they were overbearing, but they had never come close to abandoning her emotionally.

As the weeks passed, Chris became convinced that Lamar was not the man for her, and she realized that getting married would eventually harm both of them. It took her weeks to muster the courage to tell her parents. In some ways she was more nervous about telling her mom and dad than she was about telling Lamar. And she had a right to be nervous.

"They erupted," she told me later. "Dad said, 'How could you *not* want to marry him? He's a great catch. I already consider him a son.' He alluded that I was lucky to have Lamar and that I would never find anyone as good as him."

"What about your mom?" I asked. "How did she respond?"

"Well, I expected her to throw a fit, but instead she sank into her chair and mumbled something about not deserving such a coldhearted, spiteful daughter. She hasn't spoken to me since I broke the news to them—a week ago! In fact, she's hardly *looked* at me. I feel totally rejected by Mom and Dad."

I have great respect for what Chris did. The price she paid to be authentic is one that many people either can't afford or don't choose to pay. I know dozens of people who acquiesced to the "important people" in their lives and proceeded with an ill-advised marriage just to please them. The results were almost always tragic, and I promise you that contentment never accompanies this kind of inauthenticity.

■

8. THEY FEAR DISCOVERING WHO THEY REALLY ARE

Sometimes the fear of finding out who we really are, underneath all our masks and defenses, causes us to resist being authentic.

I have watched many people shrink from the pursuit of authenticity because they were afraid of the person they might discover themselves to be. In essence they say, "What if I go through all this painful work to become authentic and I don't really like who I am deep down?"

Whenever I think about this fear, I recall my Uncle Jack. He was my mother's brother, and he lived with my parents for more than fifty years. Uncle Jack was never able to make his significant romantic relationships work, and he always returned to my mother for a sense of safety. Married three or four times, Jack found a lot of acceptance with women, but his inauthentic ways always caused his relationships to break down.

Jack was a dapper dresser and a hard worker at times, but he always wanted to play life fast and free. He continually looked for a lucky break, hoping that somehow he could make it big. As you might expect, he was addicted to gambling, and he probably lost most of what he made as a house painter when he visited the racetracks every weekend.

A man of average intelligence, Jack had a gentle side with my two sisters and me and, later, our dozen children. But he kept himself entertained and preoccupied with lots of superficial activities and seldom, if ever, plowed below the surface of his life. He had virtually no emotional depth—at least none that I could detect.

I've often wondered why he worked so hard to keep from knowing who he was. Maybe he sensed that he wouldn't like the man he was if he were ever to meet up with him. What's more, my dad may have been part of the problem. Having to live around a man like my father must have been a nightmare for Uncle Jack. Dad was far more naturally gifted in intelligence, abilities, energy, and looks. If Jack was in competition with my dad, he was going to lose every time. Uncle Jack probably opted to cover up his true identity in response to his anxiety and shame.

Many people I have encountered in psychotherapy suffer the same fear. Their self-concept tends to be so thin, so poorly constructed, and so vulnerable that they prefer to remain inauthentic—even if happiness surges are their only hope for emotional satisfaction.

The tragic truth that Uncle Jack and so many like him never accept is that there is no standard they have to satisfy in order to experience lasting contentment. Uncle Jack didn't have to be as good a man, as big a man, as bright a man as my dad. He just needed to become the Jack he truly was. But he never believed he was good enough. He kept chasing after external life experiences that he thought might make up for his inadequacies. He never changed. His final years seemed to be as tormented as his earlier ones.

■

ARE YOU SAYING THAT EVERYONE HAS TO FOLLOW YOUR AUTHENTICITY COURSE TO FIND CONTENTMENT?

Some people do not even aim for contentment, but they attain it anyway. And I'm convinced that in every case it is because they are living authentically. They may use different terms to describe their authenticity or they may not use any terms at all, but they would surely fit the definition of *authentic* as I've laid it out in this book.

For all of us, this is wonderful news. When you live your life the way it was designed to be lived, whether you aim for the fullness of life or not, you will experience it. Contentment is a natural by-product of living in harmony with yourself.

I notice authenticity most frequently in children. That is, they set out quite innocently to be themselves. They usually don't consciously think, *Today I'm going to live authentically. I will be the person I was meant to be.* They just do it, and they experience the kind of unfettered joy and exuberance that older folks marvel over. It makes me sad that some adults constantly correct children and try to make them "appropriate" at the cost of their innocence and their deep state of contentment. Unfortunately, most children learn to be *inauthentic,* and they must struggle and work to regain their authenticity—which is exactly what I suspect you're doing since you're reading this book.

Having told you that some people do seem to fall into a contented state quite naturally, I must warn you that their staying there is extremely rare. Most of us must work hard to overcome these road-blocks to contentment.

Deep-down contentment and satisfaction come from being in sync with yourself. When you have never learned how to make authentic, dependable decisions, when you are a passive responder to someone else's choices, you may enjoy brief moments of happiness that come from letting others run your life, but they will soon fade. However, when you learn to make healthy choices all along the way, you set yourself up for lasting contentment.

The bottom line is that *there is no other way to arrive at contentment except by being the person you truly are.*

chapter ten

■

THE CONTENT OF CONTENTMENT

☐Imagine yourself on a white, sandy beach in Maui. It's noon on the third day of your ten-day vacation—perfect weather in the low eighties, the sweet smell of flowers in the gentle breeze, not a single thing you have to do but bask in the warm sun. You're totally free of heavy thoughts—not a nagging care on your mind. Are you content?

Imagine yourself in the kitchen of your home on a Tuesday morning. You're trying to get the kids out the door and into the car. It's your turn to drive the car pool. You have three other children to pick up, and then you have to get back home to prepare for a PTA meeting at the kids' school. After that, it's a luncheon at the church—for which you're supposed to take a salad. You have eight or ten errands to run in the afternoon, and then you'll pick up the kids at 3:15 and taxi them to soccer practice and Girl Scouts. You promised to go with your husband later to entertain out-of-town clients. You can't forget to get a baby-sitter. Are you content?

Imagine yourself in bed on a Saturday morning. It's 7:15. The weekend stretches out in front of you like an endless desert. You have nothing planned but being alone. You can literally do anything you want—stay in bed as long as you like, hop in the car and take a road trip, or curl up by the fire while you read and nap. You can call a friend to see if you can stir something up on the social front, or you can wait to see if someone calls you. Are you content?

Imagine yourself in the middle of traffic at 5:45 on a Thursday afternoon. Your day was rough, and you're frazzled. Your trusted secretary resigned, insisting that you don't pay her enough to handle such a high-pressure job. How will you ever find someone who can do all that she has learned to do? And what about this traffic? It's not even moving. You told your son that you would be there for his game promptly at 6:00, but that looks doubtful. Are you content?

Your spouse died of a heart attack four years ago, and you live alone now. Two of your children live in other states, and you see them once or twice a year. Your other daughter lives nearby, and she stops in to see you once a week. You have two or three friends you talk to on the telephone, and you almost always attend your church on the weekend. Life is very slow, and the days seem long and empty. Are you content?

You are a business executive with a packed schedule. As the CEO of your company, you're at the center of the pressure cooker. Your company has grown tremendously in the last ten years, but growth has leveled off in the last eighteen months and you fear a significant downturn. You're trying to be wise and prepare for harder times. You want to pare down the company's expenses and furlough 15 to 20 percent of your employees. This morning you are in the middle of a high-tension meeting with your executive committee, trying to decide which jobs to cut. Tempers are running high! Are you content?

■

WHEN YOU'RE REALLY CONTENT, SEAS CAN RAGE WITHOUT ALTERING YOUR INNER CALM

The quality of contentment I want you to experience makes it unnecessary to have all the external variables under control for you to feel an inner peacefulness.

Almost anybody, I suppose, could find contentment on a Maui beach under the circumstances I described. The smell of the sea air, the sound of the surf, the warmth of the sun, and the absence of any cares or concerns—these are the external qualities we most readily associate with easy-to-attain contentment. But our lives are seldom lived on golden beaches. More typically, we hurry the kids to get ready for school, negotiate with other executives about whose administrative assistant will be discharged, struggle against loneliness, or drive frantically through heavy traffic. If we can feel contented during these times, we have mastered the art of achieving and maintaining the inner serenity that makes life wonderful.

I have grown disrespectful of the "Maui approach" to contentment. Don't get me wrong, I love lazy afternoons with nothing to do, and I love Hawaiian beaches as much as anyone does. But when our inner state depends on outer circumstances, we're a long way from the deep-down, enduring contentment that can grace our lives even during the hectic and demanding days. Since the vast majority of life experiences are less than ideal, the great challenge is to learn an approach to contentment that doesn't depend on *anything* external.

■

CONTENTMENT IS THE ASSURANCE THAT EVERYTHING WILL BE ALL RIGHT

One of the most consistent killers of contentment is worry. When worry hangs like a wet blanket over the moments of your life, it suffocates contentment. But the opposite of worry is a pervasive sense that everything will work out okay. If you assume this attitude, you will maximize your contentment and be right 99 percent of the time. Research indicates that most worry is totally unnecessary, but how it does erode contentment!

When I was the dean of a graduate school of psychology, I had an administrative assistant named Marnie Fredericksen, who also became a close friend. Her life was packed full of events. Her three daughters and their families had some activity going most of the time. Social engagements, church responsibilities, and community events filled Marnie and her husband Vern's personal life. And Marnie's job kept her overloaded with a thousand details. It seemed that every student and faculty member in our school needed Marnie for something each week. The phone rang off the hook, and she had piles of mail to process.

She used to smile at me in the middle of a chaotic day and say, "Everything will be all right!" She said it from the center of her inner being. All those challenges only heightened her level of confidence. Bring on the crises—"Everything will be all right!" Let the deadlines bear down on us—"Everything will be all right!" Confront some administrative mishap—"Everything will be all right!" Whatever happened, Marnie's inner calm and self-assurance never wavered. She could smile even when all around her people's eyebrows were knit in worry and their foreheads furrowed with anxiety. Her high level of contentment was founded on her confidence, born out of her experience, that everything would turn out just fine.

■

CONTENTMENT INVOLVES THE SIMPLE CONVICTION THAT YOU'LL DO YOUR BEST

As a psychologist, I continually encounter people whose contentment hinges on achieving some goal or creating some long-sought situation. But all kinds of variables influence how our goals turn out. If your goal is to be financially free in five years, you might be set back by a health crisis that racks up thousands of dollars in medical bills. If your goal is to raise successful children, you could be foiled if they drop out of school, become addicted to drugs, and end up in jail. If your goal is to be the youngest vice president your company has ever had, you might be thwarted if the president promotes his son-in-law ahead of you. The point is, we don't have control over most variables, and that's a big reason why it makes no sense to make our contentment contingent on them.

One variable we do have control over is the commitment to do our best. This may involve our planning, our imagination, our diligence, our perseverance, and our careful use of resources. If we hitch our contentment to variables like these—the kind we *do* have control over—we stand a good chance of being contented most of the time.

I confess that sometimes I'm tempted to look straight at the bottom line to determine what my mood should be. For instance, I regularly speak to groups all over North America. I often have a clear sense of how well my speaking has gone even as I move from the podium to my chair. If my humor has failed to trigger the hearty laughter I so enjoy, my inner mood can plummet. If my most passionate and rousing points elicit only blank stares and slumped shoulders, my sense of well-being dives and my frustration soars.

But then I often look within myself and ask, *Neil, did you do your best?* I think about my preparation of the speech, my energy level during the presentation, the delivery of my material, and many other factors. And if I conclude that I did indeed do my best, I tell myself, *I did everything within my power to ensure success. That's all I could do. Nice going, my friend!* My contentment level rises like it had just received an electric shock.

All this reasoning doesn't affect my audience in the least. They, of course, would be quite surprised to know of my secret, internal conversation. But what a dramatic change it makes in me! If they go away thinking that my jokes were corny, my passion was uninspiring, and my energy level was flat, I can't do a thing about that. I did my best! Maybe I wasn't the right speaker for them. Maybe they weren't the right crowd for me. Maybe I was the ninth speaker of the day and they were restless and bored. All I know is that I did my best, and that's good enough for me.

Contentment has everything to do with how you are doing with *you*. Show me a person who is contented because he is lying on the white sands of Maui, and I will show you a person who has only a few days to be content. But show me a person who experiences contentment because he feels good about something over which only he has control, and I will show you a consistently contented person.

■

CONTENTMENT ALLOWS FOR A LONG VIEW OF LIFE AND DEATH

Dee Otte is a close friend and former associate of mine. I know her husband, Jim, only indirectly. Still, when Dee tells me about Jim, I feel that I'm intimately acquainted with him.

Jim has been going through a siege of cancer, and Dee's reports about how he is handling it have been inspiring to me. He is doing every last thing he and his doctors know to battle this incredibly challenging enemy. He goes for his examinations when he is supposed to, submits to all the necessary tests and probes, endures endless poking and prodding, and complies with sophisticated procedures.

In between the exams and treatments, Jim thoroughly enjoys all the other aspects of his life. He plays golf and helps his wife learn to love the game the way he does. He spends time with his children and grandchildren. He deepens his friendships. He participates in his church. And he listens intently to Dee as she talks about her love for him—and about her concern for his physical condition. Then when she is finished, Jim exhibits an emotional and intellectual brilliance that I find uncommon these days.

"We'll do everything we can to lick this thing," Jim says matter-of-factly, "and we'll enjoy every moment we have together. And if it should take me, I'll get an early start on heaven."

According to Dee, Jim is completely content in the middle of all this emotional and physical strain.

It strikes me that what Jim is saying is this: "Nothing—not even a potentially fatal disease—is going to rob me of the overwhelming joy of living. Life is not over until it's over, and it never will be over!" What a powerful belief this is in relation to contentment!

If I were explaining Jim's philosophy to a roomful of psychologists, there would be an immediate concern expressed about his denial defense and how it may penalize both him and Dee in avoiding their grief and discounting the gravity of the situation. But that's not what Jim is doing. In fact, he would be quick to talk about the dread he has of being separated from Dee and the rest of his family.

What Jim *is* doing is affirming a deep belief in the continuity of existence beyond the death of his physical body. This belief is grounded in his Christian faith and solidly based on scriptural teaching. And this belief is so woven into the fiber of Jim's personality that it annihilates any anxiety he would face if he ignored this faith.

I have consistently noticed that contented people have a huge time perspective. This broader orientation wrestles the threat of physical finality to the ground and pins it to the earth. It takes all the severe anxiety out of this experience with which all of us must contend on some level from birth to death.

Jim is right on all counts. This thing is not over until it's over! Let's get out to the golf course. Let's have the kids over for dinner. Let's stroll along the beach at sunset. Let's take a trip. This thing is not over yet—and it will never be over!

If you asked Jim if he is experiencing contentment, I am convinced that he would say, "To the very edges of my being!"

■

CONTENTMENT HELPS YOU SAY WITH CONFIDENCE, "I AM WHAT I AM"

Our youngest daughter, Lindsay, and her husband, Jon, have lived in Russia for several years. In some ways, it has been a grueling experience for them, but every year Lindsay seems to grow more and more contented.

"Lindsay," I said recently when I called her in Moscow, "I'm writing a book on contentment, and I want to know if you consider yourself content."

"I do, Dad. Our life is going so well, and Drew is doing well in the Russian preschool, and Mara is growing, and I have a lot of friends, and..." It was obvious from her voice that she is deeply content. Everything about the signals she was sending me was positive, and believe me, I'm a careful listener when it comes to one of our daughters who is so many thousands of miles away from home.

When I hung up the phone, I asked myself how Lindsay, living in such a tumultuous country so far from her family, could have achieved such a deep level of contentment. I thought about what a forthright person Lindsay has always been and how willing she is to be herself. And then it suddenly popped into my mind that her "senior saying" in the high school yearbook was: "I yam what I yam!" This line, of course, was first spoken so eloquently by Popeye the sailor man. At the time Lindsay decided to make this saying her "theme song," I was the dean of a graduate school. I remember feeling ill at ease at the lack of depth and the apparent self-centeredness of this proclamation.

But as I reflected on it after our phone conversation, it occurred to me that the saying represents one of Lindsay's character strengths—and one of her secrets for experiencing deep and genuine contentment. Lindsay has put her finger on a profound truth, one that makes contentment significantly more attainable.

In this book I have stressed the need for people to make consistent choices that are true to who they are. But many people fail to do this because they are afraid they need to be something different. They're not at all sure if being who they are is enough.

That's why Lindsay finds authenticity less complex. She says to the world and to all of us who know her and love her intimately, "I am what I am." It's as if she says to anyone who might pressure her to be someone she isn't, "No! I won't fall for that! I am what I am!"

People who make peace with being who they are take an enormous step toward contentment. When they are certain that this is all they need to do and be, their fundamental task in life becomes crystal clear. They are free from focusing on pleasing everyone else.

CONTENTMENT THRIVES WHEN YOU CAN FREQUENTLY SAY, "I LOVE YOU"

Literally everyone yearns to be loved, but most people are not aware that becoming masterful at loving others is central to a life of enduring contentment. Why is it so hard for us to understand the critical psychological importance of learning how to love others at a deep level? Interestingly, I have never met a person who genuinely loved many other people whose life was not overflowing with contentment.

I've noticed that when I ask friends or clients who is the most loving person they know, they often name a woman—and many of these people name a grandmother. There is something about a grandmother that triggers in our minds all the feelings of being hugged, held, and pampered. We remember her adulation and smiling that sent such a clear message of pride. We remember all the wonderful smells and tastes of holiday turkeys and pies that indicated her thoughtfulness and caring. We recall all the concern and prayers that flowed from her deep devotion to us when we were sick or passing through difficult times.

My Grandmother Clark became my mother's stepmother after Mom's birth mother died at an early age. That my stepgrandmother showed me so much love when I was a little boy seems remarkable to me. She had no genetic link to me, but she genuinely loved me. She played with me in the sandbox for hours. I remember that vividly because she was crippled with arthritis, and her being in that sandbox at all was a deep expression of her love.

Everyone knew "old" Grandma Clark as a loving woman. I never heard her say anything that wasn't tender and sympathetic. She gave generously of the few material things she owned, but what she really shared was her interest, affection, empathy, and wisdom. I believe that all of her family members sensed that she came bull's-eye close to the secret of the good life. She exuded a genuinely contented spirit.

When you become masterful at loving other people, you automatically become more and more positive in your outlook. You embrace everybody's strengths and shrug off the defects. Your smile gets wider, your ears become more attuned, and you become curious about what is happening within the heart and soul of others. You simply become intent on loving them, and suddenly, you find your life overflowing with contentment.

■

CONTENTMENT GROWS WHEN WE LEARN TO TAKE GOOD CARE OF OURSELVES

Contented people seem deeply confident that they can take good care of themselves. For instance, when I'm not out of town speaking, I work out at a local athletic club three days a week. Every time I go there I see the same people, and I observe how much they seem to enjoy their lives. Their conversations with each other sparkle. They climb on those bicycles or treadmills and seem to be going strong long after I've finished.

It appears to me that these people are highly attentive to the important aspects of their lives and not just keeping their bodies in shape. I hear them talk about their churches, family activities, social lives, and financial affairs, and even though they are an average of ten years older than I am, I sometimes wonder about what seems to fuel their unlimited energy.

As I was driving home from the gym the other day, I thought about what good friends these people are to themselves. They obviously are responsible and organized in the management of their lives, and it crossed my mind that their contentment seems at least partially the result of their self-directed kindness and sensitivity. They are the ones who see to it that their social calendars are well planned, that their spirits are well fed, and that their bodies are cared for.

Contented people can almost always say, "Don't worry, I'll take good care of myself." It occurs to me that this may be fundamental to their mastery of life and to their contentment. Maybe this is why I end every therapy session and every telephone call with someone dear by saying, "Take *very* good care of yourself!" When we master this kind of self-care, we contribute heavily to the level of contentment in our life.

■

chapter eleven

SEVEN ACTION STEPS TO AUTHENTICITY AND CONTENTMENT

Gary is a stockbroker who has been a friend of mine for years. He has attended several classes I've taught, and I know he takes his emotional health seriously. One day he asked me to lunch.

"Look, Neil," he began without hesitation, "I want to talk to you about authenticity. Every time I hear you speak or I read something you've written, the subject of authenticity inevitably comes up. I'm not sure I even know how to be authentic. I want some practical help in getting to wherever you think it is I need to go."

Gary's voice was tinged with frustration, maybe even irritation. Given the importance I place on authenticity, he had every right to be asking for this help.

"Okay, Gary," I said, "I'm going to tell you how to become an authentic person."

1. GET IN TOUCH WITH YOUR PAIN

I told Gary that I have known very few people who have made much progress in changing their lives, in moving toward authenticity, without focusing sufficient attention on their pain.

"What exactly do you mean by 'pain'?" he asked.

I said that pain refers to everything in a person's life that is experienced as a periodic or chronic problem—things that are off track, that set them on edge. Some pain is obvious; other pain has to be looked for as you would search for a hidden, malignant tumor in a person's body.

For instance, when you are going through a divorce, you know all about pain. You feel torn apart from the center to the far edges of your being. When your child gets in trouble with the law, you know what pain is. When you don't want to pick up the phone because the collection agency might be on the other end, you know about pain.

Other pain makes itself known through covert symptoms. If you drink too much alcohol, eat too much food, don't sleep well, feel stressed, or lose your temper—all of these are clear signals that pain exists somewhere within you.

Still other pain is harder to locate but just as problematic. If your life is out of balance regarding work and your closest relationships, you are almost certainly in pain. My close friend Alan Loy McGinnis has written a powerfully insightful book titled *The Balanced Life: Achieving Success in Work and Love.* He deals effectively with the conflicting allegiances that so many of us have to our careers and relationships. When we allow imbalance to occur, we either are or will be in pain.

Some people are terribly depressed, but they don't realize it. They slog through life assuming their gloomy disposition is normal in our stressful, busy society. Other people are angry much of the time, but they suppose that their boss or their spouse is to blame or they insist they're having "one of those days."

"So, Gary, the first big step on the road to authenticity is to look squarely at your pain and recognize it for what it is," I said. "Pain is virtually always a clear signal from deep within that something in your life needs to be changed. It provides all kinds of information useful in your quest to become more authentic."

"Well, I'm thinking about my own situation," Gary said, "and I'm not coming up with any specific pain. I don't have an ulcer, I don't throw temper tantrums, I'm not depressed—at least not consistently."

"Didn't you tell me a while back that you were having trouble sleeping?"

"Yeah."

"Has the problem gotten any better?"

"No, not really."

"Well, there you go. I bet when you're lying awake at 3:00 in the morning, you feel frustration or exasperation, which are mild forms of pain. It may not be acute, but it still suggests that something needs to be addressed."

"I see what you mean," Gary said.

"Sometimes it's easy to link pain with a specific cause. One of my clients, a CPA, always sinks into depression during tax season. It's clearly a matter of stress and overwork. For several months, he has to work incredibly long hours meeting with his clients, preparing their tax returns, and completing mountains of paperwork. When his schedule returns to normal, his depression lifts. Still, a lot of times *indirect* pain clearly indicates an underlying problem."

I told Gary about one of my first therapy cases. A woman reported paralysis of her left ring finger. Over the weeks, the paralysis moved to the rest of her hand and up her arm. Her physician had performed every conceivable test, but he found nothing physically wrong. One day she came in and described how her leg had suddenly become paralyzed. It had given out as she was walking down the street, and she had fallen and severely injured her knee. Apparently that scared her enough to confess something she had kept hidden from me.

"Dr. Warren," she said while looking at the floor, "I think I'd better tell you—I've been having an affair with a married man for six months."

Her life was out of sync. She was living inauthentically. Her body was sounding a loud and informative alarm. She had so much to gain from paying careful attention to her pain. In fact, when she ended her affair and began to make progress in therapy, her paralysis subsided.

I explained to Gary that people who deny or mask their pain—or simply live with it—seldom feel motivated to alter their life, to work toward authenticity. That is why it is so crucial for people to plunge into the middle of their pain, to feel it as powerfully as possible, and hopefully come to hate it so much that they will make changes.

"You see," I told Gary, "pain often results from living unnaturally, being inauthentic, trying to find a shortcut to contentment. To deny the pain or dismiss it is to discount one of the most incredible bio-logical and psychological signals in all of creation. Pain almost always contains vital clues about the need for change."

"All right, Neil, I get the pain principle. What's next?"

■

2. FIND OUT WHO OCCUPIES YOUR CONTROL BOOTH

"Gary," I said, "I talk a lot about a control booth, which I imagine to be at the center of every person's brain. You've heard me talk about this, haven't you?"

"Of course," he said. "Dozens of times!"

"Okay," I said. "Do you sense that you stand alone at the center of your own control booth?"

"Well, sometimes I do." Gary took a bite of his sandwich. I could see his mind working as he chewed. Finally, he said, "To be honest, it seems like there's always someone in my control booth with me. And sometimes, I'm not in there at all."

Gary is an honest man who is well on his way to taking the second step toward authenticity. I thought I would bring the discussion right to the moment.

"Gary, did *you* invite me to lunch today?"

"Yes, of course!"

"Good," I said. "And did *you* decide where you wanted to go?"

He shifted in his chair and said, "Yes. You know I did."

I sensed he was getting irritated with these distracting questions, so I got to the point. "You seem to be in charge of your decision making on matters like these. So when are you not in your control booth at all?"

There was hardly an instant of silence. "When my kids or my parents are involved with my life."

"Who makes your decisions then?"

"My wife makes every decision for both of us about our kids—you know, how we should discipline them, how strict we ought to be, what kinds of activities they'll be involved in. And my mother makes every decision that relates to my parents and me. Last week I told my mom I was going to be out of town on a business trip on her birthday. Birthdays are big with her. Our family *always* takes her and Dad out for their birthdays. So what did she do? She got really quiet and wouldn't look at me. She sighed a lot and acted hurt. Then a couple of days later, I talked to her on the phone and she said, 'I'm not getting any younger. Who knows if this will be my last birthday?' I ended up rescheduling the trip! It cost me extra to change the airline tickets, but I did it."

He was clearly irked, but he sounded like he had resigned himself to having other people make decisions for him.

I was impressed that Gary knew so precisely where he was "lost" in relation to his true self. Moreover, he knew who was keeping him lost—and in what areas.

■

3. GET YOURSELF LOVED— REALLY LOVED

"You're on your way, Gary," I said. "Recognizing that other people pressure you to make decisions *they* want you to make is a big step.

The next step—reclaiming your control booth—is even tougher. It requires tremendous courage. Two things have to happen: First, as we have said, you have to be acutely aware of the pain you're suffering in your current inauthentic state."

"Right. I've done that. What's next?"

"Second, you have to be engulfed by an unconditional love that ensures your emotional security under all circumstances. Without this kind of love, your fear will be too great. When you start the journey back to your control booth, all of the bartering deals you've made with people along the way must be forfeited and left behind."

"I'm a little fuzzy on this point, Neil," he said. "I mean, I like myself. I'm pretty confident and self-assured."

"That's true, but it sounds like you allow other people to place *conditions* on how you will feel about yourself."

"Huh?"

"Your mother, for instance. I suspect you felt like a lousy son when you told her you wouldn't be home for her birthday. Deep down, it probably made you feel less of yourself, like your value as a person had dropped a notch or two."

"Yeah, I guess so," Gary said.

"*Unconditional* means that it is a freely given love. It assures you that your value and worth will never diminish—regardless of what happens to you in your move toward authenticity. It offers total emotional security without any need for repayment. It is free of every kind of deal. Without this kind of love, your emotional security will always be at stake."

Gary asked all kinds of questions at this point. He sensed correctly that this love dynamic is essential to becoming authentic.

"Neil, let me ask you this. Are you saying that if I become authentic, I may be taking a big chance with the security I currently receive and experience in relation to my wife and mother?"

"That's exactly what I'm saying," I said softly, watching him carefully.

"So if I start operating out of my own control booth where my kids and parents are concerned, I could run into some trouble with my wife and my mother?"

"Absolutely."

"They might make me feel guilty, make me feel like a rotten husband and son."

"They might try."

"But the kind of love you're talking about would make it possible for me to survive emotionally even if they turned on me for trying to be authentically myself?"

"Exactly!"

"Where do I get loved like this?"

"I'm not sure where *you* will look for it. I personally get it from my faith. It's at the center of my relationship with God. In order for me to feel strongly enough that my worth and value will remain secure even if everyone else turns against me, I need to have enormous trust. I have this trust only in God."

Gary was trying his best to understand. "Neil, are you saying I have to buy into the whole Christian message in order to experience this security?"

"Actually, Gary, this is the only source for this kind of powerful love that I know about. Without it, you take a huge chance of moving to your control booth and ending up feeling totally abandoned and unloved."

Gary set down his sandwich and looked at me intently. "I think I see what you mean. If I know my personal worth, my value, is not determined by anyone else who might withdraw it, I can make *authentic* choices without worrying that others will think less of me."

Gary was processing exactly what he needed to. Our discussion made it obvious that he was gaining clarity about what he needed to change. But it was equally clear that he required some well-developed courage to begin the journey back to his true self. This courage would come only from experiencing and accepting a fundamental fact about himself: However he turned out to be in his authentic state, his value and worth would never fade—not one bit.

■

4. LOOK INWARD

To illustrate this fourth step, I told Gary about my daughter Luann, who has taught me a lot about looking inward. I remember her daily discipline of writing in her journal. She would crawl out on the end of the diving board above the swimming pool in our backyard and fill pages in her journal. No doubt she was doing lots of introspection as she wrote.

Even now, years later, she shows all the signs of a woman deeply familiar with her inner workings, even though her three young daughters keep her in constant motion. She subtly sprinkles comments into our conversations that reveal her prayers, her inner yearnings, her periodic wrestling matches with herself. Luann strikes me as unusually authentic, and I believe that her consistent, diligent efforts at turning inward have contributed substantially to her emotional health and wholeness.

You can't become authentic unless you get intimately acquainted with your inner world. And you can't get acquainted with your inner world unless you spend ample time there. Frankly, most of us spend far too little time reflecting and soul-searching.

Knowing that Gary is busy with three children and a hectic job, I suspected he didn't explore his inner world much, but again he surprised me.

"I've never been one to write in a journal as your daughter does, but that doesn't mean I avoid my thoughts and feelings. I go fishing almost every other weekend. Something about sitting in my boat out on the lake is so conducive to thinking. I review everything that's happening in my life. I chew on problems and try to figure out what's going on inside me."

"That's terrific, Gary! You're far ahead of most people in this regard. Sounds like you're ready to move on to the next step."

■

5. CAREFULLY EXAMINE ALL YOUR DATA SOURCES

"Any decision you make without gathering information from all available sources is a decision that has a good chance of being wrong," I told him. "Authenticity is all about good decision making. If you want to be authentic, listen long and hard to all your data sources—including both internal and external sources."

I told Gary about Dr. James Guy, the dean of the graduate school of psychology where I used to teach, who is a master data collector. Even though he has published dozens of scholarly articles and has established an enviable record as a teacher, Jim works hard at being a wise decision maker. I know of no one who searches for data quite so actively as Jim does. He surrounds himself with people whose opinions he trusts. He asks experts for their views, and he listens carefully as they respond. He reads widely, attends seminars, and conducts extensive research on topics related to his decision. Perhaps most important, he listens carefully to his values—all the guiding principles that come from his religious tradition, the Bible, lessons learned from his childhood, and so on.

"Where I sometimes get hung up," I said, "is trying to 'go it alone' when making decisions. At times, I don't seek out the opinions and viewpoints of significant people in my life. When this happens, I miss so much crucial insight."

At that point, Gary asked a perceptive question. "By collecting information from other people, don't you run the risk of letting them into your control booth? Some people are so forceful and persuasive that I might get bulldozed by them."

"You're right, that *is* a risk because all kinds of people would like to make your decisions for you. But if you bypass what others think in the name of standing in your control booth by yourself, your decision will be shortsighted. You have to trust yourself that only you have the right to make your final decision. And that's why it's so important to scrutinize and assess every piece of data, and this leads to the next step."

■

6. THOROUGHLY EVALUATE ALL THE DATA

"Gary, I meet hundreds of people every year, either through my counseling practice, my speaking engagements, or my daily interactions. I find that most people are not great decision makers. In fact, if we could study all of them closely, I think we would discover that this is why they seldom make much progress in changing their lives."

"So do you know anyone who is a great decision maker?" Gary asked.

"My friend Cliff is," I said immediately. "He married the right woman, chose the right career, purchased the right house, selected the right church, gathered the right friends, and raised his children wisely. In fact, I asked him the other day if he would change anything if he could do it all over again. He thought for a while and then said, 'I can't think of anything, so I guess not.'"

Gary seemed intrigued by that. "So what makes him such a great decision maker?"

"Cliff doesn't always take a long time to make a decision," I replied. "It's not that he's obsessive about decision making. But I've watched him closely for more than twenty-five years, and he invariably refuses to make a choice until he has evaluated the data carefully enough to understand it thoroughly. I think he's able to do this because he's internally secure enough that any outside efforts to hurry him have no impact."

■

7. MAKE DECISIONS DELIBERATELY, THEN LEARN ALL YOU CAN FROM THEM

"You've heard me talk on decision making and authenticity, and you know I often use couples considering marriage as illustrations. That's because I can think of no decision that's more important or more worthy of careful examination. One of the aspects of choosing a marriage partner that may be helpful to all decision making is the step-by-step nature of the decision. Under ordinary circumstances, lovers advance their relationship in steps. First they go out casually, then they 'go together,' then they get engaged, and finally they get married. This is careful, progressive decision making that, if managed properly, has every chance of leading to long-term fulfillment."

Gary nodded in agreement, so I continued.

"As a matter of fact, most decisions don't have to be made all at once—and they shouldn't be! The most important and far-reaching decisions are incredibly complex. They require a substantial amount of time to work through all the data and to summarize everything into a sound decision. So as much as possible, take each decision a little at a time.

"Then study the fit between the decision you have made and what you perceive to be true about you. If there is no harmony between the two, learn from this, and don't make the same mistake again. If your mom manipulates you into spending your Saturday running errands for her even though you *need* a day of fishing, learn from it. Evaluate your successes as well. If you think your wife is being too strict with the kids and you tell her so, learn from that too. Your goal is to make continual progress with regard to authenticity. So learn everything you can from each wise or dumb decision you make.

"It takes hard work and a lot of courage, but nothing in life is more important than becoming authentic and traveling the path to enduring contentment."

AFTERWORD

Now that you have finished reading this book about contentment, I hope you are committed to doing everything necessary to achieve it in your own life. The process of finding contentment requires courage and energy. Momentary happiness often appears easier to achieve and more immediately rewarding. But there is nothing quite so disappointing as a life given over to the frantic pursuit of happiness surges. You always end up empty and discouraged, and your hard work results in little durable gain.

But deep-down contentment offers such a different reward. When your moment-by-moment consciousness becomes peaceful and serene, when your daily expectation is that "everything will be all right," and when you discover that your life can be consistently enjoyable—even during the hard times—you will possess the most valuable quality available to human beings.

After all these years of being a psychologist, I deeply believe that contentment, more than any other emotional experience, is the reward for a life well lived.

I am painfully aware that the discovery of inner contentment is not an easy process. You have to fight against so much that you have learned from your parents, teachers, and the world in general. In a sense, you have to become a child again, recover your innocence, and discover your natural state. Bottom line, you have to become authentic. Authenticity is the *only* route to contentment.

Of all the writers in the Bible, I am most in awe of the apostle Paul. In his letter to the Philippians he said, "Whatever things are true, whatever things are noble, whatever things are just, whatever things are pure, whatever things are lovely, whatever things are of good report, if there is any virtue and if there is anything praiseworthy—meditate on these things. . . . and the God of peace will be with you" (4:8-9).

I hope you sense how much I want you to find this kind of peace and serenity. I strongly pull for you as you courageously break free from your chains and progressively become that person you truly are. As you walk this road of authenticity, may it lead you inevitably to heaven on earth.

You will know when you have arrived there. You will feel God's warm love everywhere within you. You will be wonderfully and eternally content.

■

FIVE SOLID DECISIONS

Decision making is fundamental to authenticity, so let's take a closer look at the decision-making process. Through the following examples, we'll encounter most of the crucial principles involved in making good choices.

■

SHOULD KATHY ACQUIESCE TO HER MOTHER?

For years, Kathy's mother has had the entire family at her house for Christmas Day. However chaotic it is for Kathy and her three kids, and however much Kathy's husband, Randy, has lobbied for a change, Kathy has virtually demanded that they return to her Mom and Dad's home every year. She couldn't stand how disappointed, angry, and sullen her mother would be if her plans were foiled.

But Kathy knows how frustrating Christmas Day has become for Randy and the kids. The day is always noisy, hectic, and filled with tension—certainly not the quiet, peaceful time Randy wants. Frankly, Kathy doesn't want to go to her mom's house either. Her older sister is always there with her five wild, unruly kids, and her two brothers have problems of a different sort. Her youngest brother has never married and continues to live at home. He sleeps until midday and then yells at the kids and generally expresses his opinions in obnoxious and maddening ways. Her other brother is divorced, and he sometimes brings his three kids for part of the day. He drinks too much, as does her dad, and Kathy has to walk on eggshells around her brother—as she has all her life—to avoid an explosive confrontation.

Christmas at her folks's house is not a wonderful day. But when it comes to this holiday—and just about everything else—her mother has been in charge of Kathy's control booth. Kathy is like an unarmed child in a war zone. She slips around as unobtrusively as possible.

Unfortunately, Christmas is only a symptom of deeper problems between Kathy and her mother. Even though Kathy ended up with a healthier husband, better behaved kids, and a richer life than her three siblings, she has nonetheless been a prisoner to her mother just as they were. And she has always suffered from it. She came to my office because she was depressed and chronically agitated.

We began to work on her relationship with her mother. We worked for weeks, and she made small progress. But when Kathy tried to retake possession of her control booth in little ways, her mother reacted. She was beside herself with grief—and was angry with me. She was convinced that I was unfairly turning Kathy against her. Kathy relented. She just couldn't take the pressure.

But finally, it all came down to Christmas. The day of reckoning was only a few weeks away, and Kathy felt the inevitable tug-of-war. She needed to make a decision, but she was filled with an anxiety that bordered on terror. Randy would have supported her if she decided they weren't going—in fact, both he and the kids would've given her a forty-eight-hour standing ovation. But she was overwhelmed by the challenge of handling her mother's hurt and anger.

So the process of reshaping her decision-making effort began. At the outset, we needed to get Kathy back into her control booth. We started with her current pain, and I helped her live with that pain as intimately as she could, for as long as possible. I knew she wouldn't be able to muster the courage needed in a situation like this until she recognized at a deep level how much her current way of managing life was costing her.

Then we had to rework Kathy's understanding of unconditional positive regard. She simply had to believe that her worth as a person was already established and not based on her mother's judgment of her.

This part of the process is so fundamental to any change. When you finally embrace the fact that you are a person of great value—even if you make someone else angry in your attempt at authenticity—you are well on your way toward wholeness. The massive invasion of powerful love that is required in a case like this is, in my mind, a spiritual matter. It is absolutely central to a person's faith perspective. Others may theorize that this kind of love comes from other sources, but one thing is for sure: Unconditional love must be discovered and accepted at the deepest parts of one's being before any real life change can take place.

Kathy gathered all the information she could about this decision from every external and internal source. And finally, she weighed and evaluated this information as long as was required to make a solid decision. In this regard, Kathy's values were crucial. For instance, if her allegiance to her husband was more important than other relationships, a recognition of this would influence her decision. In Kathy's case, her fear of her mother, and her repeated acquiescence to her, amounted to giving priority to her mother over her husband and kids.

The decision Kathy would make was absolutely central to her growth as a person. It had more to do with her personhood than simply where she and her family would spend Christmas Day. In fact, this decision might largely determine her emotional health, the health of her marriage, and perhaps even the health of her entire family for the rest of her life.

■

SHOULD I SLEEP IN THIS MORNING OR GET MY WORK DONE?

You may be asking, "Are all decisions as agonizing as Kathy's—as mind-boggling and relationship threatening?"

Fortunately, the vast majority of decisions are not as complex as Kathy's. But every decision deserves careful management. If you fail to take control of each decision, something will certainly take control of it for you. It may be your set of habits—how you've tended to make similar decisions in the past. Or it may be your biochemistry or mood—how you feel at the time. When you let your biochemistry run your life, you're headed for trouble. You aren't in charge of you anymore; your chemistry is. And when anything or anybody other than you is in charge of your decision making, you cannot be authentic. Your chances of being enduringly content are zero.

Imagine that you wake up some morning, and in that sleepy state in which you are deciding whether to get up or roll over and snooze some more, your brain suddenly clarifies the decision: *Do I get up and gain a little advantage on the day, or do I keep lying here until some urge more powerful sweeps across my being?*

Here is what you must understand: This decision is going to be made one way or another! You can make it consciously if you wish, but if you choose not to, it will be made by some other part of you— or by someone else.

When I face this decision, I try to stand in my control booth and say, "I and only I will make this decision." In the fuzziness of my mind, I do the following. I roll over and look at the clock. I ask myself if I have slept long enough. (Obviously, on a weekday, I can seldom afford this leisurely approach. It's more of a scramble to get to the office before my first appointment beats me there.) If I have slept long enough, this is crucial data.

I think about what I need to do. I ask myself how important it is that I get everything done. I consider how sleepy I am—whether I would like to pull the covers up around my shoulders and sink my head back down into the pillow. Then I almost always get up.

My life is so filled with responsibilities and things I thoroughly enjoy doing that I throw back the covers and attack the day. I'm frequently reminded of my friend Steve's words: "Let's go! I can sleep when I die."

Exploring this everyday kind of decision may seem a bit silly to you, but I've included it to illustrate an important principle: Decisions are made in your head continually. If you make them well, with comprehensive data collection and careful evaluation, your life is bound to be authentic.

■

SHOULD VICKY FOLLOW IN HER FATHER'S FOOTSTEPS?

Vicky was a twenty-year-old sophomore at a southern university, and the time had come for her to choose a major. She came to talk to me about her decision during her semester break. I had never met Vicky, but I had talked with her dad, a fellow psychologist, several times at professional meetings.

Vicky immediately impressed me as an exceptionally bright and engaging person. She greeted me with a big, friendly smile, and she conducted herself with a pleasant combination of informality and earnestness. Talking with her was like talking with someone I had known for ten years. She told me she had never been in counseling, but being around her dad had apparently made her comfortable with the process.

After our introductions she said, "Choosing a major is a big decision, and I'd like you to help me think it through."

"Bring me up to speed," I said. "Where do you currently stand on this issue?"

"I'm pretty sure I want to be a psychologist," Vicky said with a lot of energy. "But I'm nervous that my close relationship with my dad may be having too much unconscious influence on my choice."

There was a long pause, but I stayed quiet. I knew she had more to say on that subject.

"I may be closer to my mother in some ways, but my dad has always been the most powerful person in my life. Mom was the heart and soul of our home, but Dad carried the authority. I've always wanted to please him—and I have. He thinks very highly of me. He thinks he and I are very much alike, and in many ways we are. I'm very close to his side of the family."

Doing therapy with Vicky was a joy because she was completely open about her situation, forthcoming with her thoughts, and eager to understand all the dynamics that came to bear on her decision.

When she finished telling me all about her family relationships, I said, "Apart from your relationship with your dad, what do you think about psychology?"

"Well," she said, "I thoroughly enjoy it—at least as much as I know about it. Being around people has always been the most fulfilling part of my life. I especially like helping my friends think through their issues. I tend to see problems as puzzles that can be solved. I like kids and older people."

"Is there anything about psychology that you don't like?" I asked her.

"Well, I don't like statistics," she said, "and I don't like all the experimental courses I'd have to take for a psych major."

"Not many psychologists—at least, clinical psychologists—like that part of psychology," I said. "But are you good in math?"

"I guess so. I've always had good grades in math classes."

At that point, I needed to ask her a delicate question, one that is so crucial for potential psychologists to consider. "How would you evaluate your own emotional health?"

"I've given that a lot of thought," she said. "I've taken some personality inventories and some self-esteem tests at the university, and I've tried to look carefully at who I am. I'm not perfect, that's for sure, but I feel that I'm very healthy."

"If psychology is number one for you as a potential major, what is number two?" I asked.

"Art is a distant second for me," she said. "It's come naturally to me since I was young, and I paint a lot now. I've taken several art courses, and even though I think I could do well at it, I don't get the same meaning from it."

I saw Vicky one more time that week. I didn't want to tell her what I thought because she needed to come to her own conclusion, free of her dad or anyone like her dad. But everything I saw indicated that psychology would be an excellent choice for her. If she were to reject it because of her dad's involvement, it would be a terrible overdependence on him *in reverse*.

I saw Vicky's dad occasionally over the following months and years, and he told me Vicky had, in fact, pursued psychology. The last time I ran into him, he said that she had finished her dissertation and would soon be done with her doctoral work.

Vicky had gathered all of her data, explored it carefully, and then made her decision. I'm convinced it was a great decision, and if she makes all of her decisions the way she made that one, she will continue to be an unusually authentic person. Her life will be filled with enduring contentment.

■

FRANK HAS A CHANCE TO DO A MOVIE IN THAILAND, BUT SHOULD HE?

An actor I'll call Frank came to me for therapy two or three years ago. He needed help with his girlfriend. But in the middle of our discussions about his love life, an opportunity came up that would have a major impact on his career—and on his most important relationship.

As with most actors, Frank's career development had been erratic. He had made three or four major movies, and he had been paid well. But he had a strong personality and had definite ideas about the way things should be done, both of which don't usually go over well in the movie industry. As a matter of fact, he had lost some key roles that he badly wanted to land. Now his money was running out.

Frank's agent called one morning with a tentative part in a movie that was being shot in Thailand. It was a B movie that would require Frank to be overseas for three or four months. He would be substituting for an actor who had been seriously injured, and while the pay would be unusually good, little else about the role was attractive.

He told his agent he might be interested. Then the rush began. The agent called back to say that the producers needed to know *that day* if he would take the part. Otherwise, they would offer it to a British actor. Frank said he would tell them by the following day at noon. They agreed to wait.

I saw Frank for two hours on two consecutive days. When we started, he was almost paralyzed with the volume and complexity of his thoughts and feelings. There were so many ramifications to consider. If he took the role in Thailand, he would pass up any chance at two or three great roles he was being considered for in Hollywood. His relationship with his girlfriend would have to be put on hold for months. Who would care for his dogs? Would he be labeled a B movie actor by directors and producers? What would he do in Thailand while not working? And what about the acting classes he was taking?

I tried to help Frank organize his data. As his organization improved, new data had to be secured. For instance, Frank needed to know how his girlfriend felt about all this. He needed to get the advice of his mentor, who had given him guidance through the years. He asked his business manager to provide a breakdown of his finances if he took the part or if he didn't work at all for twelve weeks.

Once he gathered all his external data, he began to catalog his *internal* data. For instance, he did *not* want to spend three or four months in Thailand. He was extremely anxious about leaving his girlfriend at such a critical point in their relationship. He hated giving up on the possible roles. On the other hand, he desperately needed the money. And he thought perhaps the time away might give him a new perspective on his life.

All kinds of people were willing to make his decision for him. His agent thought he shouldn't go; he was giving up too much potential in Hollywood. His business manager argued that he should go; his bank account needed a big infusion. His closest friend, a fellow actor, thought shooting the film would hurt his reputation. His father, who had always considered acting a frivolous profession, encouraged him to go and see the world. Frank listened to all of this advice, but he stood alone in his control booth.

Fortunately for Frank, the person who mattered most, his girlfriend, allowed Frank to make his own decision. She hated the thought of being separated from him for such a long time, but they would talk frequently on the phone. And she could make sure that his house and dogs were cared for.

Frank agonized, but when he finally made his decision, he told me he felt incredibly calm. He felt peaceful and confident about his choice because he had taken all his data into account. He had listened long and hard to his thoughts and feelings and to the thoughts and feelings of every crucial person in his life. Then he stood in the middle of all this data, and he decided to go.

I could fill pages with everything that happened for Frank as a result of that decision. But here's the bottom line: *He* made the decision— thoughtfully and decisively. Consequently, he contributed substantially to his own authenticity. And over time, he repeated this decision-making process dozens of times—probably thousands of times—and he has become a man who would tell you straight out today that he is wonderfully content with his life.

■

SHOULD I GO TO RUSSIA OR NOT?

Our daughter Lindsay and her husband, Jon, have lived in Moscow for more than five years. After they had lived there only a year, my wife decided to visit them. Marylyn wanted to see Russia for herself. Jon and Lindsay were able to visit us in California three or four times a year, and while I thoroughly enjoy being with them, I had no interest in going to Russia.

But Marylyn really wanted to go, and so did our close friends Nell and Howard Privett. In subtle but powerful ways, the three of them began to pressure me. I looked ahead and saw that one of three things would happen: I could go happily; I could go unhappily; or I could refuse to go. It was crucial for me to make a careful and competent choice, because if I went, I wanted to do so with the enthusiasm that comes from knowing that my decision to go was an authentic expression.

I collected all my data. Some of the external data was easy to assemble. Marylyn *badly* wanted to go, and I knew that she would be delighted if I shared her excitement about the trip. On the other hand, I had a manuscript due, and there was no way I could go without violating the publisher's (and my own) deadline. Moreover, I had some speaking engagements I would have to cancel, which I hate doing.

Internally, I found myself resisting more travel. *I spend enough time on planes as it is,* I told myself. *And besides, I detest the effects of jet lag.* I wasn't excited about seeing Russia. I thought of it as old, decayed, dangerous, and boring.

Then came my internal counteroffensive. I knew that Russia is rich with custom and tradition. Called the "richest country on earth," I kept thinking about the pictures of Khrushchev reviewing the troops while overlooking Red Square. And I thought how wonderful it would be to see where Lindsay and Jon live.

For three weeks, I walked back and forth in my data. I was totally stuck! But one day I told my secretary and close friend, Dee, about my ambivalence.

She asked me an absolutely brilliant question. "Out of all your considerations, which one is more important than any other? I mean, which one strikes you as having the most long-term meaning to you?"

The answer came immediately to my mind and through my lips: "The fact that Marylyn wants to go so badly, and the fact that she wants so badly for me to go with her. That stands out above all other considerations."

"Well," Dee said, looking me straight in the eye and talking slowly, "then that strikes me as a very important point. But if you decide to go, remember why you're going, and go with enthusiasm."

It struck me that Dee had suddenly become my psychotherapist!

My decision, pondered so endlessly through the weeks, was finally made on the spot. I had gathered the data, I had made sure *I* was in my control booth, I had scrutinized it thoroughly, and I had considered my values (how the trip would enhance my relationship with Marylyn).

I went to Russia—enthusiatically. And it was a wonderfully enriching time.

Decisions come fast and furiously. I am arguing that if you take on the challenge of personally handling this part of your life—and if you learn to do it with great skill—your movement toward enduring contentment will be swift and steady. You simply cannot end up being content at the center of your being if you fail to make solid choices at every point along the way.

NOTES

1. David G. Myers, *The Pursuit of Happiness* (New York: Avon Books, 1992).

2. Ronald Inglehart, *Culture Shift in Advanced Industrial Society* (Princeton: Princeton University Press, 1990).

3. William J. Bennett, *The Index of Leading Cultural Indicators* (New York: Simon & Schuster, 1994), p. 8.

4. Norma Zamichow, "Enjoying a Real Life, Unplugged," *Los Angeles Times*, 26 October 1996, p. 1.

5. Neil Clark Warren, *Finding the Love of Your Life* (Colorado Springs: Focus on the Family Publishing, 1992).

ABOUT THE AUTHOR

Neil Clark Warren is one of America's best known relational psychologists with thirty years in his own practice. He received his bachelor's degree from Pepperdine University, his Master of Divinity degree from Princeton Theological Seminary, and his Ph.D. in clinical psychology from The University of Chicago. In addition, Dr. Warren is a much sought after speaker who captivates listeners with his ability to passionately relate complex issues in a simple, practical, and easily understood format.

Dr. Warren's first book, *Make Anger Your Ally*, was heralded a "must read" by *Time* magazine. His *Finding the Love of Your Life* was an international bestseller and the 1993 recipient of a Gold Medallion award for Best Marriage book. Warren is also the author of *The Triumphant Marriage*, selected in 1995 by *USA Today* as having made an outstanding contribution to the field of marriage.

A frequent guest on national television and radio programs across the country, Dr. Warren and his wife, Marylyn, live in Southern California. They have three grown daughters.

For more information regarding Dr. Warren and his books and seminars, call (626) 795-4814.